STRATEGIC*finance*

COMMONFUND
AND
TIAA-CREF ASSET MANAGEMENT (TCAM)
MADE GENEROUS CONTRIBUTIONS
TO THE DEVELOPMENT OF *Strategic Finance*

STRATEGIC *finance*

Planning and Budgeting
for Boards, Chief Executives, and Finance Officers

BY KENT JOHN CHABOTAR

**Association of Governing Boards
of Universities and Colleges**
One Dupont Circle • Suite 400
Washington, D.C. 20036

Strategic Finance: Planning and Budgeting for Boards, Chief Executives, and Finance Officers

Copyright © 2006 by Association of Governing Boards of Universities and Colleges, One Dupont Circle, Suite 400, Washington, D.C. 20036.

Printed and bound in the United States of America.

Library of Congress Cataloging-in-Publication Data

Chabotar, Kent John.

Strategic finance : planning and budgeting for boards, chief executives, and finance officers / by Kent John Chabotar.

    p. cm.

Includes bibliographical references and index.

    ISBN 0-9754948-7-2
    1. Universities and colleges — United States — Finance. 2. Universities and colleges — United States — Business management — Planning. 3. Educational fund raising — United States. 4. Universities and colleges — United States — Administration. I. Association of Governing Boards of Universities and Colleges. II. Title.

LB2342.C363 2006

378.1'06 — dc22

                                    2006029685

This publication is intended to inform discussion, not to represent or imply endorsement by AGB or its members.

For more information on AGB Publications or to order additional copies of this book, call 800/356-6317 or visit our Web site at *www.agb.org*.

STRATEGIC *finance*

Planning and Budgeting
for Boards, Chief Executives, and Finance Officers

●●●●●●●●●●●●●●●●

CONTENTS

Strategic Finance

*Planning and Budgeting for Boards, Chief Executives,
and Finance Officers*

By Kent John Chabotar

PREFACE

Higher education has become considerably more complicated since 1958, when President Clark Kerr of the University of California made his famed remark that "the three major administrative problems on a campus are sex for the students, athletics for the alumni, and parking for the faculty."[1] In the ensuing half-century, America's political and economic environment is far less stable, and our society's needs and desires have changed markedly. Consequently, in the higher education realm, strategic planning and budgeting have become central issues for presidents and boards.

Defining an institution's fundamental purpose, vision, and core values, its environment and markets, and then deciding what long-term strategies and tactics are needed to fulfill a vision for the near and distant future are the hallmarks of strategic planning. The essence of strategic budgeting lies in raising money through earning, borrowing, or investing funds and then allocating the resulting income among virtually unlimited competing and pressing needs.

Less clear in many organizations is the connection between strategic planning and budgeting. Strategic plans often are flawed and unaffordable because they contain incomplete or inaccurate financial information about current and projected costs and revenues. Rarely are financial decisions based explicitly on an institution's mission and goals. Budget decisions are made in a short-term strategic vacuum that not only fails to advance the plan but also wastes money in the long run. Capital campaigns with dollar targets related to institutional priorities are as close as many colleges and universities ever get to strategic budgeting. With planning in many institutions proceeding from the top down, and budgeting from the bottom up, such gaps are hardly surprising.

The origins of this book lie with a seemingly innocent e-mail, the subject line of which read: "An AGB 'Opportunity.'" Tom Longin, former vice president of programs and research at AGB, wrote to ask me to write a book on finance that was connected to institutional strategy. I was well acquainted with AGB, having taught the Seminar for New Trustees and other workshops at the National Conference on Trusteeship and having coauthored an AGB Board Basics booklet, "Financial Responsibilities." The central challenge in writing the book, Tom suggested, was to explain how, in an increasingly turbulent environment, colleges and universities could embrace a strategic vision and sense of direction that enhanced academic

---

[1] Clark Kerr. (Inaugural speech for the University of Washington's new president, Charles E. Odegaard.) *Time Magazine* Archives, November 17, 1958.

programs and student services while maintaining a balanced budget and investing in human and facilities capital.

The resulting chapters of this book focus on strategic planning, budgeting, and the linkages between them. It assumes that the essential prerequisite of a successful, strategy-focused college or university is the strong connection among the strategic plan, long-range financial plan, and the annual budget. Here is a summary of the chapters:

- **Chapter 1: Making the Case for Strategic Planning and Budgeting.** Strategy is about setting basic directions—sometimes involving radical change and risk—that allow the institution to deal effectively not only with internal priority setting and budgeting but also such environmental challenges as demographics and state and federal government policies.

- **Chapter 2: The Strategy-Focused Organization.** A strategy-focused college or university links financial decisions both to its mission and strategic direction. Major goals and priorities are not accepted without knowing their full costs. Such institutions consider the multiyear program and financial plan to be the starting point for the annual budgeting process and recognize that faculty and staff commitments are needed for the strategy to succeed. They obtain external benchmarks from competitors and others rather than focusing only internally. A strategy-focused organization understands that change is inevitable and thus maintains flexibility by developing "what if" scenarios and contingencies. Finally, the strategy-focused institution or organization persistently evaluates assumptions, outcomes, and actual revenues and expenses and uses these data to improve planning and budgeting.

- **Chapter 3: Strategic Planning: Contexts and Ends.** Colleges and universities must base strategic planning on their core values or on fundamental beliefs such as academic excellence or diversity. Strategic planning considers the environment and the specific issues or opportunities that affect the institution, both internally and externally. From these considerations emerge the overarching mission statement that articulates the institution's renewed basic purposes and reasons for being. The mission is accomplished through more concrete goals and specific objectives.

- **Chapter 4: Strategic Planning: Evaluation and Means.** Strategic planning entails the identification and evaluation of strategic indicators that measure how well objectives are being accomplished. Evaluation of whether the plan is on time and on budget occurs when the plan is assessed in terms of progress toward objectives, goals, core values, and mission. The means of a strategic plan are the action steps that specify who is to do what, by when, and with what resources in order to achieve the ends of the plan.

- **Chapter 5: Strategy and Budgets.** The budget flows from the strategic plan and the long-range financial plan that supports it. The major goal of budgeting is to realize financial equilibrium. This involves balancing budgets (operating, cash, and capital), constraining endowment spending, and investing in salaries, maintenance, and other priorities. Balancing the budget depends on critical decisions about tuition pricing, inflation, endowment earnings, employee salaries and fringe benefits, maintenance, and other variables.

- **Chapter 6: The Budgeting Process.** It matters how the budget is prepared. Colleges and universities use processes that are increasingly consultative and even participative—often through a budget committee representing faculty, staff, and students. The president and the board, however, have final approval of the budget, regardless of the level of other constituent participation.

- **Chapter 7: Budget in Crisis: Coping With Financial Distress.** Colleges and universities periodically endure difficult financial circumstances when enrollment or state appropriations drop, budget commitments are overextended, or other financial stress factors come into play. To restore financial equilibrium, institutions have various mission-driven revenue and expense options ranging in phases from the least painful, such as deferring expenses, to the most difficult, such as closing programs.

- **Chapter 8: The Strategy-Focused Organization: A Case Study.** The fictional but plausible case of "McKinley College" ties together and applies the many principles set forth in the book. Relevant principles are discussed using four broad categories—financial analysis, strategic planning, strategic budgeting, and retrenchment. The case is analyzed in terms of what McKinley's administrators and trustees did, or should have done. The case analysis draws on the real-life reactions of participants studying the case in AGB's Seminar for New Trustees.

Trustees oversee and approve rather than "do." Formally and visibly, trustees must support the strategic planning process and endorse the involvement of all campus constituencies in its development, especially the president and senior leadership. The board's most important responsibilities in this regard are to ask good questions, establish broad financial principles to help guide the administration, and ensure that decisions related to the annual budget and facilities follow the plan.

Change *is* indeed inevitable. During the many months of discussions, research, focus groups, and thinking and writing that led to *Strategic Finance*, I moved from the position of chief financial officer at Bowdoin College in Maine to that of president of Guilford College in North Carolina. (Readers will notice that I have drawn many examples from these institutions.) I especially wish to acknowledge the contributions of four focus groups comprising trustees and financial officers from public and independent institutions who provided insights and practical advice on how the book might best meet their needs. Without the aid of Courtney Tolmie and Pat Vardaro, student research assistants at Bowdoin College, executive assistant Joyce Eaton at Guilford College, and especially Merrill Schwartz and Deanna High, patient and supportive AGB editors, this effort would not have seen the light of day. Many thanks to everyone.

Kent John Chabotar
Greensboro, N.C.

CHAPTER 1

Making the Case for Strategic Planning and Budgeting

It was the best of times, it was the worst of times, it was the age of wisdom, it was the age of foolishness, it was the epoch of belief, it was the epoch of incredulity, it was the season of Light, it was the season of Darkness, it was the spring of hope, it was the winter of despair, we had everything before us, we had nothing before us....

— CHARLES DICKENS

THE OPENING OF *A Tale of Two Cities* might properly characterize higher education in the 21st century. On one hand, colleges and universities have proved to be significant contributors to economic growth, social mobility, innovation, and personal income. Increasing proportions of the population in almost every demographic category seek college degrees. American higher education generally is regarded as the best in the world. Yet higher education is also viewed as inefficient, overextended in majors and programs, elitist, wasteful, and too expensive. Students and families struggle to afford a college education despite increasing amounts of financial aid as colleges and universities face escalating pressures from federal and state governments for more accountability, lower costs, and better safety and health.

In response to these and other challenges, most colleges and universities focus merely on better marketing of the status quo and on incremental changes — striving to increase revenues, cut expenses, streamline operations, and improve communications based on a one-to-three-year time horizon. Some institutions do better. They try to act strategically by identifying their areas of distinction and core competencies to transform programs and services. Over five or more years, they curb random growth, reallocate budgets and staff to align with institutional mission, balance current and future needs, and assess performance with a focus on outcomes. In so doing, these institutions tether their vision and long-range plan to time, money, space, and other realities of the institution and its environment.

This chapter seeks to make the case for *strategic* planning and budgeting rather than the usual incremental or operational approach. It shows how a strategically focused institution can set new directions and priorities, encourage fundamental change, and become more effective and efficient. This view argues that strategic planning and budgeting allow the institution to adapt to events and circumstances in the external environment.

Benefits of Strategic Planning and Budgeting

Almost everyone in higher education has witnessed the following: A college or university enthusiastically embarks on a strategic planning process. After a year or two, the chief executive and trustees announce a "bold and new" strategic plan. Promises are made about linking the annual budget to the new strategic plan going forward. The public-relations effort is enormous. Press releases inundate every local media outlet, brochures are distributed, articles appear in the student newspaper and alumni magazine, and the plan appears on the university's Web site. Implementation of the plan begins with a flurry of activity and a few early achievements, after which nothing much happens as the strategic plan slowly fades and disappears in institutional memory.

For every institution that embarks on a strategic planning process, the costs in time and money are large, and the risks are great — even if participants follow the principles and practices this book suggests for planning and budgeting more effectively. So why should colleges and universities go down this road, given that success is far from guaranteed? The answer is that the benefits of strategic planning and budgeting are enormous. They include the following:

· The creation of a framework for long-range thinking and organizational change;

· An increased appreciation for, and use of, data in decision making;

· Enhanced knowledge of marketplace perceptions of the institution, its competitors, and ways to secure competitive advantage;

· The setting of basic budgetary priorities for the institution's programs and services;

· A sense of urgency and excitement that encourages academic and administrative constituencies to work together to accomplish goals;

· An improved understanding of and dialogue about the institutional vision that fosters a sense of ownership in the strategic plan and the university;

· Budget decisions linked more to mission and core values than to last year's budget or available revenue; and

· Assessment and adjustment of the organization's responses to changing environments.

In short, strategic planning is a disciplined effort to produce fundamental decisions and actions that shape and guide what an organization is, what it does, and why it does it — all with a focus on the future.[1]

---

[1] Adapted from Alexandra L. Lerner, *A Strategic Planning Primer for Higher Education* (College of Business Administration and Economics, California State University, Northridge, July 1999); and John M.M. Bryson, *Strategic Planning for Public and Nonprofit Organizations: A Guide to Strengthening and Sustaining Organizational Achievement*, (San Francisco: Jossey-Bass, 1995).

Strategic Choices

Financial concerns ordinarily drive strategic planning and budgeting. Colleges and universities quickly realize that long-term financial viability cannot be ensured merely by adding more students, increasing tuition, securing new donors, and obtaining more government support — especially in a time when successfully dodging major cuts in state appropriations is deemed a victory. Viability also is not guaranteed by cutting existing staff, departments, and programs or even by selective outsourcing of admissions and tuition-management services.[2]

Unless the institution has been financially promiscuous, reducing expenses has diminishing returns and soon begins to threaten academic quality and attractiveness. In turn, this erodes admissions and development. What needs to change in fundamental ways is not the budget but the institution itself. What are examples of such basic strategic choices?

1. Adding or dropping an entire population of prospective students.

· A private college embarks on a successful adult-education program and an early college program for gifted high school students that eventually surpasses by more than half the enrollment of the student body.

· An urban university establishes satellite campuses to expand enrollment and add graduate programs via distance education.

· A community college reduces enrollment in order to improve selectivity and to focus on fewer majors with broader appeal.

2. Adding or dropping entire programs.

· An undergraduate college decides to add graduate programs in collaboration with local public universities.

· A land-grant university adds a law school in the state's largest city to serve underrepresented populations.

· A private college sells its law school in order to focus on undergraduate education.

3. Focusing the curriculum.

· A comprehensive university restructures curriculum and its reputation around innovative uses of instructional technology.

· A liberal arts college embraces the "practical liberal arts" by adding preprofessional programs and expanding internship and service-learning opportunities.

4. Changing the mission.

· A two-year state college becomes a four-year institution by offering professional programs in nursing and criminal justice.

---

[2] Robert C. Dickeson, *Prioritizing Academic Programs and Services* (San Francisco: Jossey-Bass, 1999), p. 127.

· Despite burgeoning enrollment, a residential liberal arts college decides not to add capacity to its residence halls and dining services in order to avoid more debt and to capitalize on higher retention rates from off-campus students. By assuming that two-thirds or more of students will live off campus, the college essentially transforms itself into a commuter school.

Strategic planning and budgeting engages the interest (and sometimes the opposition) of faculty, students, and others far more than does incremental tinkering with mission or finances. It elevates the vision of all participants, encouraging them to reflect creatively on the strategic directions of the institution. It is dramatic, somewhat precarious, and almost certain to leave the institution in a different state. Even conversations about strategy that challenge the status quo have the potential to upset longstanding relationships and decision-making processes — even if the strategy is not altered. Finally, strategic thinking encourages a dynamic chief executive and governing board to be bold and unconventional in considering institutional transformation.

Here are three examples of institutions that illustrate the point:

Boston College. When Father J. Donald Monan, S.J., assumed the presidency in 1972, Boston College was approximately $30 million in debt, its endowment was less than $6 million, and faculty and staff salaries had been frozen during the previous year. Rumors about the university's future included speculation that Harvard University would acquire it.

Father Monan set into motion the university's upward trajectory in finances, reputation, and global scope. His first priority was to reconfigure the board of trustees. By separating the board from the direct influence of the Society of Jesus, Monan was able to bring in the talents of lay alumni and business leaders who helped turn around the college's fortunes. He cultivated government leaders who were also Boston College alumni, such as U.S. House Speaker Thomas P. "Tip" O'Neill. In 1974, Boston College acquired Newton College of the Sacred Heart, a 40-acre campus only a mile or so away. This addition allowed Boston College to expand its law school and provide more housing for a student population that was increasingly residential and geographically diverse.

When Father Monan left the presidency in 1996, Boston College's endowment had grown from $5 million to nearly $1 billion; the number of countries represented in the student body had risen from 34 to 91; and faculty salaries had soared from an average of $17,025 to $82,000. In Father Monan's 24-year administration, Boston College averaged more than one new building a year — O'Neill Library, a renovated stadium, and several residence halls were key additions. Today, Boston College has one of the most selective admissions processes in the United States.[3]

Chatham College. Chatham is one of the oldest women's colleges in the country. Its Pittsburgh campus incorporates the former estate of financier and industrialist

---

3 Wikipedia, "Boston College," *en.wikipedia.org/wiki/Boston_College* (accessed August 23, 2006). See also: *www.bcheights. com/media/paper144/news/2000/05/02/Features/*

Andrew Mellon. In 1993, Chatham's enrollment had fallen from nearly 700 students to 623 — not enough for long-term survival. Appointed in 1992, President Esther Barazzone revitalized the college with a comprehensive strategy to stimulate growth in the undergraduate program, expand the college's continuing education and master's degree programs, add sites, cut expenses, and eliminate the deficit.

Barazzone initiated campuswide centers for innovation — including the Center for Women in Politics in Pennsylvania, the Pittsburgh Teachers Institute, and the Global Focus program. She also guided the college through the addition of more than 40 traditional undergraduate programs, and in a bold move, opened the continuing education and master's degree programs to men. In harmony with debt reduction and enrollment growth, Barazzone initiated successful fund-raising campaigns to help invigorate the campus.

Perhaps most crucial to Barazzone and her plan was the board's trust in her leadership. Board members met directly with the college community in a series of "visioning" exercises that sketched the challenges and the opportunities of change. The board also restructured its bylaws to affirm the president's authority relative to the board and the faculty.[4]

Arizona State University. Upon his arrival from Columbia University in 2002, Arizona State University President Michael Crow announced plans to transform the institution into the country's leading urban research institution. Crow worked to expand the size and scope of Arizona State while simultaneously raising its quality. He asserted that Arizona State would measure its success not by the proportion of students it rejects but by the educational attainment of the students it accepts. To accommodate the state's soaring college-age population (many of whom are minority-group members from low-income backgrounds), Crow announced plans to increase enrollment, already the nation's fourth largest, by 56 percent — from 61,000 to 95,000 — by 2020.

As state support for higher education dropped, Crow expected ASU to become more entrepreneurial and to double the research budget with new funds from government agencies, foundations, and the private sector. In conjunction with this last strategy, Crow claimed that Arizona State would revive downtown Phoenix and help diversify the region's sluggish low-tech economy, which historically relied on the "the five C's — cattle, cotton, copper, citrus, and climate."[5]

These three leaders epitomize strategic thinking in a number of ways. Finances played a major role in prompting their institutions' shifts from incremental change to radical transformation. New sources of revenue were identified to replace traditional reliance on student fees (at Boston College and Chatham College) and state appropriations (at Arizona State University). Each of these presidents also decided to focus attention and resources in specific areas: Monan on the law

---

[4] Michael K. Townsley, "Back on Track: Small College Turnarounds," *Business Officer* (September 2002) *www.nacubo.org/x2421.xml*; and Allen P. Splete (ed.), "Presidential Essays: Success Stories," (Indianapolis: Lumina Foundation, 2000), p 2.

[5] John L. Pulley, "Raising Arizona," *Chronicle of Higher Education* (November 18, 2005), pp. A28-30.

school, Barrazone on centers for innovation, and Crow on research and urban redevelopment. Monan and Barrazone have transformed their institutions — in finances and reputation among other characteristics — and Crow has the same intention. Especially at Boston College and Chatham College, institutional change would not have occurred without the help of the trustees in ways such as recruiting new trustees, encouraging innovation, and supporting the president.

The Strategic Environment

What are the major societal, economic, technological, and structural issues that affect colleges and universities? An awareness of the leading issues helps frame the strategic plan, the long-range financial plan, and the annual budget. Knowledge of the operating environment also provides urgency to strategic planning in terms of persuading an institution to deal with the issues instead of risking surprise or assuming a reactive or defensive stance.

The issues to consider are timeless — demographics, affordability, financial aid, consortia and collaborations, information technology, intercollegiate athletics, community involvement, and standards and accountability — but they offer a way to focus attention not only on competitive pressures but on the need to reconsider mission and markets. The following brief examination of these issues will give texture to board discussions:

Demographics

Surging Enrollments. College and university enrollments are rapidly increasing with dramatic variations among groups and regions. Attendance has grown so rapidly that 75 percent of high school graduates now receive some postsecondary education within two years of receiving their diplomas.[6] Total college enrollment is projected to grow from 16.4 million in 2004 to 18.1 million in 2013.[7]

Moody's Investors Services has described positive demographic trends in the traditional student population of 18 to 24 year-olds as "the key stabilizing factor in private higher education."[8] Yet the number of adult students (25 and older) has grown markedly in recent years, with numbers approaching one-half of all undergraduates. In addition, college enrollments will be increasingly non-white and non-Hispanic. By 2018, for example, Hispanic students will constitute a larger proportion of Arizona's high school graduating classes than will white students.[9]

Geographic, Gender, and Sector Variation. Geographically, the West will grow the most, with high school graduates in that region expected to increase significantly in the coming years. Exhibit 1.0 illustrates the expected percentage change in high school graduates by states through 2018.[10] A gender shift is occurring, too, with

---

[6] Association of American Colleges and Universities, *Great Expectations for College Achievements* (Washington, D.C.: 2002), p. viii.

[7] *Chronicle of Higher Education Almanac* (August 26, 2005), p. 18.

[8] Moody's Investors Service, *Private Colleges and Universities Outlook and Medians 2002-2003* (June, 2002), p. 6.

[9] Ben Gose, "Questions Loom for Applicants and Colleges," *Chronicle of Higher Education* (February 25, 2005), p. B-10.

[10] Western Interstate Commission for Higher Education, *Knocking at the College Door* (WICHE, 2003), p 23.

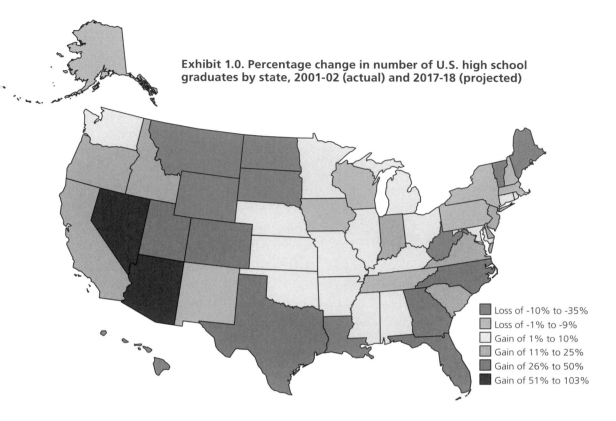

Exhibit 1.0. Percentage change in number of U.S. high school graduates by state, 2001-02 (actual) and 2017-18 (projected)

Loss of -10% to -35%
Loss of -1% to -9%
Gain of 1% to 10%
Gain of 11% to 25%
Gain of 26% to 50%
Gain of 51% to 103%

women now accounting for nearly 60 percent of all college students compared with 40 percent in 1961.[11] In terms of educational sector, the U.S. Department of Education reports that enrollment in public higher education institutions will go from 12.9 million in 2006 to 13.9 million in 2013, while enrollment in private institutions will rise from 3.9 million in 2006 to 4.3 million in 2013.[12] Finally, the importance of international students — with related emphases on international business, challenges of globalization, and study-abroad programs — continue to impact enrollment and curricular programming. In 2004-05, the number of international students enrolled in U.S. higher education institutions remained fairly steady at 565,039 — off about 1 percent from the previous year's total, according to Open Doors 2005, the annual report on international academic mobility published by the Institute of International Education (IIE).[13]

Faculty Retirement. Demographics also affect faculty employment. Higher education faces a generational shift as professors from the Baby Boom generation near retirement age. Nearly one-third of full-time professors are now 55 years old or older. Although public universities and community colleges experienced a surge in faculty retirements in the late 1990s, recent market declines may slow retirements, as faculty no longer can count as much on accumulated capital gains in their pension portfolios.

---

[11] Association of American Colleges and Universities, *op. cit.*, p. 2.

[12] *Chronicle Almanac 2005*, p. 18.

[13] "Report on International Educational Exchange," *www.opendoors.org?p=69736* (accessed July 11, 2006.)

Strategic Issues. Strategically, colleges and universities must address several issues about the demographic wave. How will demographic trends affect their own enrollment and that of their principal competitors? Will these trends affect enrollment in various programs within the institution differently? If larger enrollments are likely, what are the effects on financial aid, academic and social space, and numbers of faculty and staff? Will the number of faculty need to rise more slowly than the number of students, thus driving up the student-faculty ratio, in an effort to save money and enhance efficiency? With endowment per student a significant indicator of financial strength, especially at independent institutions, how much will adding more students dilute this ratio if the stock market stagnates?

Affordability and Financial Aid

Cost and price are not synonymous terms. The cost of an education is what the institution spends to educate students and to perform other functions, such as pay faculty salaries, purchase laboratory and computer equipment, construct buildings, and maintain the campus. Price is the published rate of tuition and other fees (often including room and board) that often is reduced by financial aid.

College Costs. College costs rise despite the demands of government and business leaders for improved productivity and the complaints of students and parents. Colleges make huge capital investments in physical and human resources not simply to expand the student body or produce more graduates but to become better at educating students. The real cost of educating a student at comparable public and private institutions is virtually the same. Differences are insignificant in terms of what colleges and universities on the same level of prestige and quality pay for salaries, benefits, utilities, travel, facilities, and other goods and services. The major difference in the price charged to the student is due to the state appropriation that uses tax dollars to reduce the price students pay to attend public institutions.[14]

D. Bruce Johnstone, professor at the State University of New York at Buffalo, has argued that costs in higher education are virtually immune to productivity savings. He notes that technology is used not to save labor costs but to add value, that the imperative for recognition and prestige is significant, that market demand for better accommodations and more services is real, and that prices routinely are discounted to attract academically talented and economically disadvantaged students.[15] The student-faculty ratio is a classic example: Seeking to enhance quality, colleges spend more to lower the ratio and, in an economic sense, lower productivity.

Sticker Price. The average sticker price (before the application of financial aid) for student fees between 1986-87 and 2005-06 rose about 200 percent at four-year private institutions and 220 percent at four-year publics. Public demand for higher education drives up prices — as it does in any competitive market. In round numbers, a college diploma earns an annual return — after accounting for inflation — of

---

[14] National Association of Independent Colleges and Universities, *Behind the Price Tag* (Washington, D.C., 1998), pp. 2-4.

[15] D. Bruce Johnstone, "Fiscal Future of Higher Education: Austerity and Accessibility," speech presented at the Pullias Lecture Series on the Future of Higher Education, University of Southern California (Fall 2003).

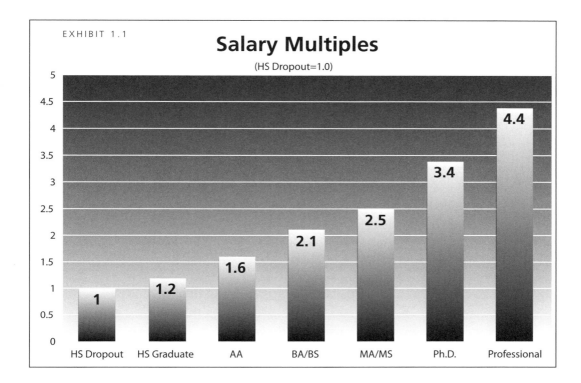

EXHIBIT 1.1

Salary Multiples
(HS Dropout=1.0)

13 percent to 14 percent on its cost that far exceeds the long-term returns on stocks or bonds.[16] On average, the higher a person's educational attainment, the higher his or her annual household income. As shown in Exhibit 1.1, the annual income for a person with a college degree is almost double the income for a high school graduate who did not go to college. The gap widens to greater than four times salary when a business, law, or other professional degree is earned.[17]

Financial Aid. Increasing "net tuition" — the amount left over after institutionally funded financial aid — is a prime concern at most colleges and universities that seek financial stability. For decades, the percentage growth in total financial aid per student was higher than the percentage growth in total tuition and fees; grant aid has grown more slowly than loans.[18] (About two-thirds of undergraduates receive some form of financial aid — grants, loans, and campus work.[19]) The average discount rate — institutionally funded financial aid as a percentage of tuition and fees — has been about one-third at elite independent institutions in the top 50 in *U.S. News & World Report* college rankings and well over 40 percent for other institutions.[20] The classic conflict in financial aid is balancing student recruitment with economy. Colleges and universities try to attract a student

---

[16] Susan Lee and Daniel Roth, "Educonomics," *Forbes* (November 18, 1996), pp. 108-116.

[17] S. Baum and K. Payea, *Education Pays 2004: The Benefits of Higher Education for Individuals and Society* (New York: The College Board, 2004), p. 11.

[18] Lord, *Trends in Student Aid, op. cit.*, p. 5.

[19] *Ibid.*, p. 4. See also: Richard Ekman, "Private College Aid Cuts Tuition in Half," from "Letters to the Editor," *The Wall Street Journal* (October 28, 2002), p. A19.

[20] Lucie Lapovsky, *Tuition Discounting and Prudent Enrollment Management*, AGB *Priorities* (Fall 2004), p. 4.

body of desired size and diversity with targeted merit- and need-based aid. At the same time, they seek to constrain financial-aid spending funded by their operating budgets (as opposed to government sources and endowment). This concern is greater at lesser-endowed institutions such as Guilford College, where only 13 percent of institutional financial aid is drawn from endowed sources. At more highly endowed colleges, such as Bowdoin, the endowment in 2002 paid about 50 percent of the cost of institutional financial aid. Although such economy may have negative consequences on enrollment, every dollar saved in budget-funded financial aid is another dollar available for spending on other strategic priorities.

Student Borrowing. A 2005 survey by the Partnership for Public Service found that college seniors and graduates feared "going deeply into debt" and "being unemployed" more than they feared being attacked by terrorists.[21] As William Strauss, coauthor of *Millennials Rising* and other books about Americans born since 1982, notes: "This is a larger issue than many people realize. It's altering life directions. Rather than pursuing academic paths, [students] feel much more obliged to pursue the highest paying corporate path. That is a significant change from 30 to 40 years ago."[22]

Full Cost and Student Fees. Finally, in all but the most tuition-dependent colleges and universities, no student pays the actual full cost of education. If an institution's budget is funded 70 percent by student fees (tuition, room, and board) but 30 percent from other sources, such as government aid, endowment earnings, and gifts, the average student receives a 30 percent subsidy. At Guilford College, the sticker price for tuition and fees in 2006-07 was about $30,000 per student. Yet, because student-fee revenue supported "only" 80 percent of the budget, even students who received no financial aid (also known as "full pays") received a 20 percent subsidy on a total cost of education of around $37,500. Aided students, with an average institutional aid award of $12,000, had a total subsidy approaching 50 percent of the total cost. College presidents and boards do not communicate this fact often enough to concerned parents and students.

Strategic Issues. One of the most complex sets of relationships in higher education is among college costs, tuition prices, financial aid, and enrollment. While most colleges and universities seek to contain their costs and limit their price increases, they also worry about the extent to which internal and external economics will affect financial aid and the diversity of the student body. Student-aid packages are composed of grant, loan, and work subsidies, all which must be calibrated to hit sometimes contradictory goals: a targeted enrollment size and diversity and maximization of net tuition. Setting the price of tuition and other fees has potential strategic impacts on competitiveness, public image, funding, and quality. Boards will need to study how tuition and aid policies affect enrollment.

Consortia and Collaborations

Many colleges and universities are cooperating in various areas in an effort to offer more programs and services together than each can offer alone or to gain cost efficiencies. Such collaborations were once limited to allowing students

---

[21] Greg Toppo, "Graduates fear debt more than terrorism," *USA Today* (May 19, 2005), p. 8D.
[22] *Ibid.*

to cross-register for courses at other institutions. Today, this practice has become routine, while many institutions have moved on to sharing administrative services and overhead costs.

In their 1999 book on best practices for consortia, L.G. Dotolo and Jean Strandness discuss four conceptual approaches to collaborations:

1. **Share the risk.** Colleges may choose to share various forms of insurance, including property and casualty, liability, life and health, and worker's compensation.

2. **Share the resource.** This type of collaboration usually occurs in functional areas such as equipment, libraries, service contracts, faculty, and administrative staff.

3. **Do unto and for others.** One consortium member provides a service to the others for a fee that is especially attractive when one institution is much bigger. (There are some caveats, however, as the providing institution may have to pay unrelated business income tax.)

4. **Expand your bargaining power.** Large-volume purchases can increase bargaining and reduce costs. Utilities, supplies, services, and software are cited as prime examples.[23]

In exploring cost effectiveness, many colleges distinguish between cutting costs and avoiding costs. Cutting costs is an attempt to deliver the same service more economically. For example, two of three colleges in a consortium decide to eliminate their philosophy departments and related faculty positions. Avoiding costs adds or expands a service but at a lower cost per institution; for example, three colleges together hire and share one new faculty member with a specialization in the philosophy of Hegel.

The organizational management of consortia ranges from a series of informal, bilateral arrangements with no separate staff to legally incorporated entities with a large centrally staffed office.

Strategic Issues. Setting complementary tuition and fees, conducting effective program assessments, and managing and funding the consortium are among the important considerations with potential strategic consequences. The trade-offs involved often concern balancing the financial advantages associated with consortial programs with the loss of autonomy and control. The strategic impacts are also different if an institution uses the consortia to chart a new direction rather than to maintain existing programs and services. For example, an undergraduate college collaborating with a state university to offer joint graduate programs essentially has changed its mission.

---

[23] Lawrence G. Dotolo and Jean T. Strandness, *Best Practices in Higher Education Consortia: How Institutions Can Work Together: New Directions for Higher Education, No. 106* (San Francisco: Jossey-Bass, 1999).

Instructional Technology

Technology presents great opportunities and grave dangers to colleges and universities; success depends on skillful management of resources. Although technology has become an integral part of many professions and disciplines, it is still finding its way in the classroom setting, where traditional teaching techniques such as lectures and seminars predominate. Increasingly, the Internet and other advances in information technology are prompting colleges and universities to view *instructional opportunities* on three levels.

1. Level I involves the use of *productivity tools* such as word processing, presentation, spreadsheet, and other software for student and faculty research and writing. All institutions today are equipped to function on this basic level.

2. Level II centers on *how* institutions teach and use technology to allow asynchronous learning — learning that occurs at the student's own pace and often outside the traditional classroom (to facilitate the viewing of works of art, for example). At Level II, interaction between instructors and students via e-mail, bulletin boards, and chat rooms as well as online completion of assignments enhance classroom learning and communication. Most institutions are reasonably proficient at this level.

3. Level III involves changing *what* is taught; fewer colleges and universities have succeeded in implementing technology at this level. In teaching accounting, for example, technology has allowed a shift away from rote memorization of debits and credits to a greater focus on what the numbers mean and how to act on them.[24] Colleges and universities have strategic choices about the level to which they aspire. Hardware and software costs rise as each level is reached, both in initial investments and in continuing support costs. Less obviously, the cultural shifts required to change *how* institutions teach are minor compared with the transformation needed to change *what* is taught. Institutions should avoid the "one size fits all" trap of assuming that the same level is appropriate for all programs.

Distance Education and Other Applications. Many postsecondary institutions offer at least some courses by distance education, and a few have such programs for specialized degrees and professional schools. Distance education is a complex strategic and financial issue. It has evolved rapidly, raised questions about reporting and organizational structures, and prompted debates about applications for classroom and administrative uses. Distance education has encouraged new and strengthened competitors in the higher education marketplace. The University of Phoenix and other proprietary institutions have pioneered on-demand education with superb curricula and faculty, targeting older and employed students.

Colleges and universities use information technology not only to improve instruction but to reduce instructional costs. For example, Ohio State University redesigned its core statistics course by reducing the time students are required

---

[24] Conversation with President Joe Morone, Bentley College (March 2002).

to spend in class and substituting a variety of online components relevant to specific majors. Campus officials estimate that the change reduced the cost of offering the course by 31 percent, while it opened up 150 new classroom slots.[25] On the administrative side, technology in the form of sophisticated modeling and presentation software also may facilitate strategic decision making.

Strategic Issues. EDUCAUSE, an organization that monitors information technology in higher education, conducts an annual survey that has perennially identified funding as the first or second most significant strategic issue in information technology. Related strategic concerns include (1) the availability, currency, and performance of administrative software and the capabilities of staff to manage these systems; (2) the strategic value of information technology to enhance teaching, learning, research, and service; and (3) systems security.

Intercollegiate Athletics

The role of athletics is a primary strategic and financial concern at many colleges and universities. At the competitive NCAA Division I and I-A institutions, issues surrounding intercollegiate athletics can be pervasive, especially since most big-time sports programs do not make enough money to cover their costs. What's more, an athletics "arms race" among the big-time programs — which has fostered new arena and stadium construction and aggressive currying of corporate sponsors — has led to public skepticism about the integrity of intercollegiate programs at the national level.

Beyond this are issues concerning gender balance in accordance with Title IX, the adequacy of fitness facilities for nonathletes, and the impact of fielding competitive athletics teams on admissions practices. Even Division III schools track "rated athletes" in the admissions process, as well as grade points and graduation rates for both men and women.[26]

Strategic Issues. The centrality of the athletics program influences the strategic plan and budget in many ways. Boards will need to examine the effects of athletics on costs, student recruitment and quality, academic programming, and public image. These effects will vary among institutions depending on the division and conference of NCAA competition and the number and kinds of teams (intercollegiate, club, and intramural). Which teams, if any, are self-supporting and which require a subsidy from the athletics department or elsewhere in the institution?

Sports teams are a natural link between the institution and its alumni, and the quality of the relationship can affect their financial support. Boards will need to determine the extent to which capital gifts may be restricted to the athletics program (or even particular sports) and may need to consider other policies regarding support for intercollegiate athletics.

---

[25] William Symonds, "Colleges in Crisis," *Business Week* (April 28, 2003), pp. 72–79.

[26] William G. Bowen and James L. Shulman, *The Game of Life: College Sports and Educational Value* (New York: Mellon Foundation, 2001).

Community Involvement

An institution's relationship with its surrounding community is multifaceted. Service on nonprofit boards, membership in civic and professional organizations, payments in lieu of taxes, and internship and service-learning opportunities are just a few of the kinds of general areas of commitments. Two aspects of community involvement have especially significant strategic implications for colleges and universities: their relationship with K-12 education and their economic impact.

Relationship with K-12 Education. Higher education is becoming more involved with elementary and secondary education. Teacher training has always been a familiar curricular component, though institutions lately have emphasized a need to balance pedagogical preparation and substantive knowledge.

The rise of charter schools and experimental privatized approaches has complicated the linkages that colleges and universities have had with both public schools and independent schools. Questions arise about K-12 involvement in terms of the adequacy of preparation of college-admitted students and the proliferation of "early college" programs for gifted pupils. "We want to make sure that there is a consistency between what the students are required to do in order to graduate from high school and what we're requiring for admissions," asserts Judith Gill, chancellor for higher education in Massachusetts.[27] Some institutions make the strategic choice to set admissions standards that ensure that new students can be successful without extensive remedial work. Others — with enrollment challenges — will admit students of varying abilities from high school and use orientation and introductory courses to prepare them more effectively for college-level work. Still others will become directly involved in K-12 education through expanded teacher training programs, consulting assistance, and early admission of gifted high school students.

Economic Impact on the Community. Compensation paid to faculty and staff, purchases to support the academic program and student life, and money spent in local businesses by students and visitors are often cited as examples of the economic impact of colleges and universities on the local community. Public institutions, especially, have commissioned studies to show legislators and citizens how much value they add to the state and local economies. Some examples:

- In Michigan, public universities asserted that they contributed nearly 13 percent of the state's gross product — or $39 billion. For each dollar the state spent on higher education, according to the study, Michigan's economy got $26 back.

- A University of Wisconsin report maintained that the university generated 70,000 state jobs and contributed $4.7 billion annually to the state's economy.

- The University of Arizona reported that its receipt of $285 million in grants, contracts, and gifts paid for 3,500 jobs and that its total research expenditures accounted for $384 million in statewide sales.[28]

---

[27] Lynn Olson, "K-12 and College Expectations Often Fail to Mesh," *Education Week* (March 9, 2001).

[28] Will Potter, "Public Colleges Try to Show Their Value to States, But Not Everyone Is Convinced," *Chronicle of Higher Education* (May 9, 2003), p. A26.

The strategic issue here is not the economic impact *per se*. Every institution from community colleges to research universities provides jobs and other economic benefits to their communities. Rather, the issue is how much the institution prioritizes the economic well-being of its region or state in its strategic plan, how academic and administrative programs are reshaped to that end, and the effect of this decision on existing instructional, service, and research activities.

Strategic Issues. Local communities expect that colleges and universities will be sensitive to their concerns. One challenge for campus officials is to be aware of the economic impact of the institution on the community — especially if local demands for payments in lieu of taxes escalate. The strategic plan should state the priorities of community involvement and set forth specific programs and services or a process for making those decisions. Allowing community involvement to be decided at only the departmental level can result in unnecessary spending, shift attention from the mission, and risk political or social controversies.

Standards and Accountability

Besides granting degrees that qualify graduates for employment and additional education, what else does higher education accomplish? Columbia University President and Nobel Laureate Nicholas Murray Butler once argued that the five evidences of education included speech, manners, reflection, growth, and the ability to act.[29] The measurement of outcomes as a justification for curricular and extracurricular choices, tuition and fee payments, and support from governments and foundations has evolved from a debate among scholars to a requirement for reaccredidation. For example, the Southern Association of Colleges and Schools' state institutions are required to meet the following standard for reaccreditation: "The institution identifies expected outcomes for its educational programs and its administrative and educational support services; assesses whether it achieves these outcomes; and provides evidence of improvement based on analysis of those results."[30]

Accountability for results affects presidents and administrators during annual evaluations and faculty in their tenure reviews. Trustees should be concerned with how well the institution evaluates its curriculum, tracks how students acquire the knowledge and attributes the institution deems important, and assesses how well alumni feel their education prepared them for later life.[31]

Strategic Issues. Colleges and universities must become more serious about assessment of student outcomes, faculty and administrative performance, and other strategic priorities. The establishment of evaluation criteria, sources and uses of data, and methods for using results must be stated in the strategic plan. Assessment processes can be expensive. Budgeting for measurement and evaluation may require new funding or budget reallocations even from mission-critical programs.

---

[29] Quoted in *The Forbes Book of Business Quotations* (New York: Leventhal, 1997), p. 227.

[30] Southern Association of Colleges and Schools, *Principles of Accreditation: Foundations for Quality Enhancement* (Decatur. Ga., 2001), p. 22.

[31] Kathryn Mohrman, "What Matters in the Liberal Arts," *Trusteeship* (July/August 1999), pp. 8-12.

Yet the demands of the public, accrediting bodies, and lawmakers for increased accountability and transparency make assessment as mission-critical as anything else the institution undertakes.

Increasingly, chief executives and boards in higher education resemble ship captains trying to steer their institutions through both calm seas and maelstroms. Demographics, affordability, and financial aid present as many opportunities for creative thinking as they do challenges. The shoals on which institutions can founder are numerous and sometimes hidden. Strategic budgeting and planning provide a direction to a college or university tantamount to using a compass and sextant. Chief executives and boards have used these tools not only to successfully sustain their present course, but also to chart wholly new directions that inspire confidence and motivate effort at all levels of the institution.

CHAPTER 2

The Strategy-Focused Organization

A strategy-focused organization centers its finances and other components on its mission and goals. It evaluates issues and opportunities not only for short-term effectiveness but also for how they affect basic directions and values, markets and customers, and the preservation of human, financial, and physical assets. A strategy-focused organization also involves its key stakeholders in the development and implementation of the strategic plan and budget.

This chapter outlines the main characteristics of a strategy-focused college or university in answer to the following questions: What principles does the organization follow in planning, budgeting, and management? Which specific kinds of institutions have special opportunities or problems in becoming strategy-focused? What are the roles of the chief executive, chief finance officer, the board, faculty and staff, students, and other stakeholders and constituency groups?

Principles of a Strategy-Focused Organization

A strategically focused organization endeavors to do the following:

1. **Link financial decisions to the mission and strategic direction of the organization.** Undoubtedly, budgeting and other aspects of financial policy are more relevant if the institution has a mission or strategic vision that sets goals for instruction, research, and service. The board can state this vision in a formal plan with a mission statement, continuing and specific objectives, and definite programs and assignments of responsibility. It also can be organic, developing and changing over time and supplemented by periodic statements of intermediate-term academic or administrative priorities. Such clear ends for the institution — whether formal or informal — are essential ingredients for programming and budgeting the most effective means. As *Alice's Adventures in Wonderland* reminds us: "If you don't know where you're going, any way will get you there."

2. **Determine the total costs of major goals and priorities.** A strategic plan may be elegantly designed with a logical flow from the mission to the ultimate ends, incorporating the appropriate programs and strategies needed to accomplish them. Yet plans often fail when the price tag is seriously underestimated or even unknown. The costs of new majors, innovative programs, expanded departments, additional staff, and investments in businesslike enterprises seldom are properly calculated or summed to arrive at a total cost for the plan. Such a total cost includes not only the direct costs of staff and operating expenses but also the overhead costs of administration and facilities that can add 20 percent or more to direct costs. Included in, or resulting from, the strategic plan is the campus

master plan that lays out needed construction and renovation, classroom and office space, and land use. An institution must not implement its plan until the necessary resources have been identified and at least partly secured.

3. **Link the annual budgeting process explicitly to the multiyear program and financial plan.** The initial year in the long-range financial plan constitutes the first draft of the annual budget. If the financial plan properly documents all costs, it will have forecast revenues and expenses over five or more years. The plan's forecasting assumptions must be lucid and convincing, taking into account inflation, annual fund and capital campaign expectations, levels of state appropriations, and formula funding.

On the revenue side of the ledger, tuition and fees are the largest source of funds at most institutions; thus, it is crucial to project accurate enrollments, admissions acceptance and yield rates, retention rates, and financial-aid discounts. State appropriations are a major — but often diminishing — source of revenue for public institutions and difficult to forecast given the complex economic and political factors that drive them. In addition, investment returns and expected new gifts will influence the amount of endowment spending that will be possible. The most common rate is 5 percent of the endowment market value averaged over the prior two to three years.

The most significant expenses for most institutions are salaries and wages, expenses that depend on projected numbers of faculty and staff linked to the strategic plan, pay increases, and benefits costs. Authorizing a bond issue to fund construction commits the institution to pay debt service over many years, though state authorities sometimes relieve public colleges and universities of this burden. A capital project also obligates the institution to a consistent maintenance program that competing needs must not supplant.

4. **Pay attention to the human resources needed for the strategy to succeed.** Strategy is as much about people as it is about money. Key constituencies must be involved in the formation of any plan or change in strategic direction. Genuine participation not only improves the quality of the final plan but also fosters understanding and acceptance. To accomplish this, the workloads and schedules of participating staff and students may have to be accommodated.

As planning evolves, deans and directors must be accountable for the programs and tasks assigned to them — and for results. The essence of performance management is that everyone knows how their work contributes to the organization's larger purposes. Ask yourself: Do we have the organization and personnel to manage our finances effectively? Do we provide enough training and technology? Have we linked our human resources and succession planning with the phases of our strategic plan? Is the reward system consistent with our values and goals?

5. **Promote benchmarking and market comparisons.** No strategy exists in a vacuum. A strategic plan pays close attention to the environment and the

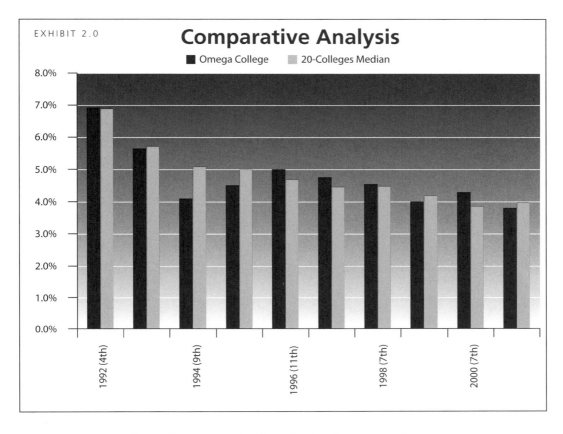

EXHIBIT 2.0

Comparative Analysis

■ Omega College ▨ 20-Colleges Median

interests of significant stakeholders. It also focuses on the competition. Endowment returns — among the most highly benchmarked data in higher education — have different asset classes and markets with short-term and long-term averages to which individual returns can be compared. Virtually every college or university formally or informally also compares itself with other institutions in terms of admissions selectivity, student fees, and employee salaries. A strategically focused organization does this systematically.

Exhibit 2.0 illustrates a comparative analysis of student fees, contrasting the average annual percentage increases in student fees between "Omega College" and its 20-college comparison group between 1992 and 2001. As shown in the brackets beneath the fiscal year notes on the exhibit, Omega's rank within the 20-college group has been as high as second and as low as fourteenth over the period.

Why is this important to know? Although small differences in fees between competing institutions do not influence student choices about where to apply and enroll, large and growing differences might. Additionally, the more dependent the institution is on student-fee revenue to fund its budget, the less likely it will be able to achieve one rank for total fees and annual increases and another, significantly higher or lower rank, for faculty salaries, spending on athletics, and other priorities. "Leaving money on the table" is a favorite expression of budget makers when they realize that their percentage increase in student fees is much

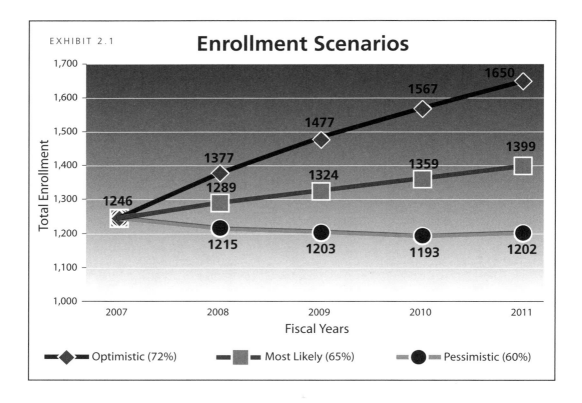

EXHIBIT 2.1

Enrollment Scenarios

Legend: Optimistic (72%), Most Likely (65%), Pessimistic (60%)

X-axis: Fiscal Years — 2007, 2008, 2009, 2010, 2011
Y-axis: Total Enrollment

Data points:
- 2007: 1246
- Optimistic: 1377 (2008), 1477 (2009), 1567 (2010), 1650 (2011)
- Most Likely: 1289 (2008), 1324 (2009), 1359 (2010), 1399 (2011)
- Pessimistic: 1215 (2008), 1203 (2009), 1193 (2010), 1202 (2011)

lower than the competition's, and the difference could have been used to support academic and administrative services more effectively without endangering enrollment. Finally, there is the public-relations challenge of the need to explain to parents and other constituents why student fees were raised by the chosen percentage and how these rates compare with those of peer institutions.

6. **Maintain flexibility by developing "what if" scenarios and contingencies.** A strategy-focused organization views its assumptions as influenced by events and circumstances as well as by internal decisions to increase revenue or cut costs. Interest rates and endowment returns can rise and fall; government regulations can impose new burdens; local, state, or national administrations can turn over; and a host of factors can upset even the most diligently constructed plans. Thus, the organization must make tentative decisions on how it would react to the unexpected — before it occurs. If state appropriations dropped 10 percent, how would the university respond? Where would a college increase revenues or cut costs if endowment returns were 0 percent rather than 7 percent?

Exhibit 2.1 exemplifies a "what if" analysis for enrollment. Scenarios are built around "transition ratios," or the percentage of students continuing from prior semesters plus new first-year students and transfers. Estimates of enrollment, student-fee revenue, number of faculty and staff needed, and other prime budget drivers emerge from each scenario. For example, at a 16-to-1 student-faculty ratio, each 16 students added in the scenario is equivalent to one faculty member, more or less. All scenarios start at 1,246 students and assume the same number of first-year students and transfers with the same steady increases throughout the period. The differences arise from the transition ratios that are based on the most recent four-year average.

Set at the four-year average, the most likely scenario assumes the current transition ratio around 65 percent, which peaks enrollment at 1,399 in the 2010-11 fiscal year. The optimistic scenario increases that ratio to 72 percent, which was the case ten years earlier. In this scenario, enrollment reaches 1,650. The pessimistic scenario sets the transition rate at 60 percent, in which enrollment struggles to 1,202, or 37 percent below the optimistic projection.

7. **Persistently evaluate assumptions, actuals, and outcomes.** A strategy-focused organization is continuously analytical. Strategic indicators, qualitative and quantitative, tether all levels and phases of the plan to reality. What are the most substantial sources and uses of funds, and how have they changed? What are the expectations of tuition or endowment income as revenue sources, and have they changed in recent years? Targets and acceptable variances are established that allow the institution to monitor progress, identify variances, and take corrective action. The results are recycled throughout the organization to shape the plan, annual budgets, organization structure, endowment and investment decisions, and personnel appraisals.

Strategic Planning and Budgeting: Special Challenges and Opportunities

Three types of institutions have special challenges in becoming strategy focused. Many of these challenges relate to finances. Institutions with large endowments lack the financial incentive to make tough strategic choices. In a sense, they can afford to do almost everything. Small institutions — perhaps using NACUBO's definition of 850 students and below — center their strategic attention on maintaining enrollment and often lack the resources to manage endowments and undertake bold initiatives. Strategic planning in public institutions is limited by the vision of the governments that fund and control them, a scenario that has been complicated by eroding public appropriations and thus greater dependence on student fees, other earned income, and fund-raising.

Institutions with Large Endowments. Highly selective, well-regarded, elite colleges and universities spend large amounts from their endowments and charge high prices to support academic and co-curricular programming of increasing apparent quality and prestige. At such institutions, between 15 percent and 40 percent of the annual budget may depend on endowment earnings. Students and parents view the high price of tuition and other fees as an investment that will be paid back over a lifetime.

This popular linkage between wealth and excellence is not unfounded, based on the annual college and university rankings in *U.S. News & World Report*. An extraordinarily strong correlation persists between endowment size and *U.S. News* ranking.[1]

---

[1] David F. Swensen, *Pioneering Portfolio Management* (New York: The Free Press, 2000), pp. 18-20.

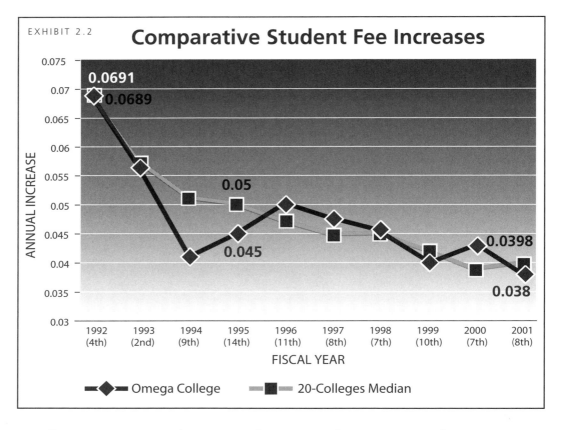

EXHIBIT 2.2

Comparative Student Fee Increases

Systematic strategic planning rarely occurs at elite institutions. Since strategic planning involves complex choices among competing directions and priorities, well-endowed colleges and universities tend to want to "do it all." Budgeting is easier when comparatively little is needed from student fees or state appropriations. Still, no institution has unlimited resources, and expectations often rise to meet income levels. This means that not every campus constituency receives what it wants or needs (or claims it needs). Many higher education veterans marvel that rich and poor institutions often have the same debates about priorities and scarce resources.

Dependence on endowment does have challenges, however. Spending rates are questioned as either too high to preserve the endowment's long-term purchasing power or too low to relieve budgetary dependence on student fees. Large endowments often are capable of sustaining their commitment to targeting high returns with more volatility and higher risk through investing in venture capital, hedge funds, and other alternative asset classes. As a result, large endowments consistently earn better returns than smaller endowments.[2]

Small Institutions. Small institutions have fewer students over which to spread overhead costs, and economies of scale are marginal or nonexistent. Most academic

[2] Mimi Lord, *Trends and Issues: Highlights of the 2005 NACUBO Endowment Study* (TIAA-CREF Institute, 2006), pp. 2,5; John L. Pulley, "Another Downer of a Year for College Endowments," *Chronicle of Higher Education* (January 24, 2003), pp. A23–A27; Greg Winter, "College Endowments Post Solid Gains in '04," *New York Times*, Web edition (January 24, 2005).

departments and administrative offices are thinly staffed so that the addition or deletion of even one position is a proverbial "big deal."

In terms of endowment spending, small colleges may lack the information systems and staff needed to utilize fully restricted endowment funds for the operating budget. Although Bowdoin College, for instance, had developed a database to identify available funds for particular purposes, such as financial aid restricted to Maine residents, college officers still relied on the memories and experience of long-time staff members. Institutions with small endowments face other problems, too, such as when to diversify beyond one or two outside managers — often one for equities and the other for fixed income — educating the investment committee in the distinctive responsibilities of investing a nonprofit's endowment, and determining the role of trustees who have professional investment expertise.

A small institution especially needs to determine its areas of excellence because its priorities truly are expressed in its budget. At the same time, such institutions must budget flexibly because they depend so heavily on net tuition and fee revenue to finance operations. Unless it belongs to the small minority of well-endowed and highly selective institutions, a small independent college's budget is very sensitive to swings in enrollment and financial aid. Institutions in these circumstances typically do not finalize their budgets until the fall — when actual enrollment is known.

Public Institutions. Strategy at a public institution often reflects the need to compete with other state colleges and universities and with other governmental institutions for sufficient budget support. It also may reflect the agenda or priorities of the state government or higher education system. Responsibility for budgeting may be dispersed and driven by certain funding formulas.

Historic reliance on state appropriations has allowed public colleges and universities to keep student tuition and fees for in-state students 20 percent to 50 percent lower than at comparable independent institutions. Until recently, most public institutions have had scant incentive to raise money through private gifts or endowment growth. But with the widespread erosion of state funding, public institutions have sought other sources of support, often redoubling efforts to increase research grants and annual giving. Many have focused much time and attention on increasing capital giving and growing endowments, and are using institutionally related foundations to gather and manage assets. Occasionally, this has led to tensions between governing and foundation boards in articulating institutional priorities for philanthropic giving.

Constituent Responsibilities

Because a strategic plan sets the fundamental direction and priorities of the institution, its development and implementation should involve the entire community. Such an approach not only acknowledges the "constitutional" roles of various groups in making major decisions but also improves the plan's feasibility, transparency, and degree of acceptance. The need to involve the governing board, chief executives, and other senior officers is widely recognized, though not the precise nature of that involvement. How should faculty staff, and students participate? How can alumni be helpful? What roles should be considered for consultants and government officials?

Chief Executive. The president or chancellor is responsible for leading the planning and budgeting processes. Regardless of on-campus support or outside assistance, the chief executive has to be the "planner-in-chief" and "budget czar" if anything truly effective is to happen. Among the most important tasks of the chief executive are the following:

· Determining the need for planning.

· Designing appropriate processes for planning and budgeting.

· Obtaining permission from and cooperation of the board, system office, or other superordinate bodies.

· Providing a "charge" for planning and budgeting that spells out institutional priorities.

· Engaging vice presidents and deans in leadership roles and ensuring their active support and participation.

· Hiring consultants, especially to facilitate board involvement and to develop the campus master plan.

· Communicating — formally and informally — during the process to determine progress and the satisfaction levels of various constituencies.

· Ensuring that the process is timely, widely participative, and focused on the core needs of the institution.

· Working with staff and trustees to connect the strategic and financial plan to endowment and investment management.

· Leading the effort to raise current and capital gifts and government aid to support the plan and budget, with an emphasis on unrestricted giving where possible.

Dennis Jones, president of the National Center for Higher Education Management Systems (NCHEMS), has argued that public institution leaders have special obligations in strategy and budgeting. First, leaders must imbue budgets with incentives for behavior that contribute to implementation and achievement of plans. Second, they must ensure that the institution's human and physical assets are sufficient, well maintained, appropriate to the mission, and responsive to the needs of key constituents, particularly the state. Finally, leaders must make certain that the institution is buffered against unexpected financial misfortune by budgeting flexibly and establishing contingency funds.[3]

Governing Board. A governing board's fundamental responsibility is to chart the institution's course and ensure that the institution has the resources it

---

[3] Dennis Jones, *Strategic Budgeting: The Board's Role in Public Colleges and Universities*, Occasional Paper No. 28 (Washington, D.C.: AGB, 1995).

needs to fulfill its mission. The board also has a unique fiduciary role in finance and budgeting, in endowment and investment management, and in preserving and expanding physical resources. In addition, boards ordinarily are called on to participate in fund-raising activities in support of the plan.

While the board's financial and fiduciary responsibilities are complex and extensive, its basic responsibility is to oversee and govern the institution rather than manage it. Day-to-day management of the institution properly belongs to the chief executive and his or her administration. Working with the chief executive and others on strategic planning and budgeting, the board contributes best by doing the following:

- Promoting a long-term perspective that focuses on the ends to be achieved: What do we want our university to become? How will we know when we are successful?

- Ensuring that the institution complies with applicable laws and regulations, including protecting its tax-exempt status.

- Reviewing and approving the strategic plan, financial plan and underlying assumptions, and resulting annual operating budgets.

- Preserving the institution's facilities and making capital decisions by authorizing construction, issuing bonds, and ratifying the purchase or sale of any property.

- Monitoring and overseeing, directly or by delegation to committees and professional staff, the institution's investments and endowment.

- Guiding the institution's fund-raising and other development efforts and participating in those efforts through personal contributions.

- Endorsing the strategic and financial plans with legislators, foundations, the media, and other agencies that shape public opinion or supply funds.

- Establishing risk-management policies, including adequate insurance coverage, checks and balances over the institution's senior officers, and annual disclosure of trustee possible conflicts of interest.

Board Committees. Multiple board committees are involved in the strategy-focused college or university. To be sure, the full board signs off on the strategic plan and its underlying assumptions. But as the work of the board often occurs at the committee level, so too do many of the components of the strategic and financial planning processes. During the process, the chief executive, chief finance officer, and other appropriate senior administrators should consult often the various committees and the chairs about the major budget components and campus concerns.

- The academic affairs committee oversees the central purposes of instruction and research. New degree programs, curricular shifts, and tenure — with its implications for institutional flexibility and faculty recruitment — are among this committee's top concerns.

- The growing importance of admissions and retention emphasizes the roles of board committees that deal with admissions, financial aid, and student life. These topics may fall under the purview of different committees at various institutions, but often they are the responsibility of the student affairs committee. This committee also often handles the deepening complexities of intercollegiate athletics. Some boards now have enrollment management committees to coordinate enrollment efforts previously scattered among other board committees.

· The finance committee reviews the financial assumptions and especially the long-range financial plan, annual budget, and proposed debt financing. The finance committee's chief role should be to contemplate how various budget options affect not only next year's budget but also the institution's long-term financial outlook. For example, what will be the impact in ten years of an annual spending rate of 5 percent of the endowment's market value?

· The investment committee is also crucial to strategic planning. It works through the chief financial officer to integrate its work with the finance committee so that financial strategy meshes with endowment and investment management.

· The development or advancement committee should endorse any fund-raising targets and be solidly engaged in achieving them. Members form the nucleus of any capital campaign steering committee.

· The facilities committee (often called buildings and grounds) oversees campus master plans, major maintenance, and building construction and renovation.

Professor Regina Herzlinger of the Harvard Business School has developed four questions that can help board members develop a strategic sense of their role and a system of measurement and control to ensure optimal organizational performance.[4]

1. **Are the organization's goals consistent with its financial resources?** Many colleges and universities adopt strategies and plans they cannot afford. This arises when plans are adopted before they are adequately researched, or when the institution relies on overoptimistic projections of new revenues and fund-raising. A few institutions have excessively modest goals relative to their resources.

2. **Is the organization practicing intergenerational equity?** Contrary to Benjamin Franklin's aphorism, colleges and universities can "escape death and taxes." As tax-exempt, charitable entities, they for the most part pay no taxes and often outlive multiple generations of students, faculty, and alumni. A strategic perspective acknowledges that the institution must balance short-term and long-term needs and wants. For example, not spending on maintenance frees up money for other priorities for the short term but imperils long-term building integrity and financial equilibrium when the deferred maintenance "bill" comes due. A high endowment spending rate might satisfy today's needs, but the benefits may come at the expense of

long-term endowment growth and the needs of future students. A very low rate, conversely, may speed long-term endowment growth, but it may impair development of critical academic and administrative programs.

3. **Are the sources and uses of funds appropriately matched?** Colleges and universities should not make long-term commitments based on short-term grants or unstable revenue sources. Depending on a three-year research grant to support a tenured faculty member indefinitely is as imprudent as using one-time gifts to fund new programs or increases in staff compensation. Relatively fixed expenses should be funded by fixed revenues — for example, the funding of debt service for a dining hall using revenues from student board fees.

4. **Is the organization sustainable?** Usually, if the answers to the first three questions are satisfactory, the institution can maintain programs and services at current levels. Sustainability is not just an institutionwide issue; in a large university it may apply to specific colleges and schools. For example, in the late 1980s, Harvard's overall financial strength did not prevent its Graduate School of Design from experiencing problems that led to severe reductions in budgets and staffing. Sustainability is enhanced by effective strategic planning linked to long-range financial plans and annual budgets, diversification of revenue sources, and not investing too much of the budget in one or two programs that may become vulnerable.

Chief Financial Officer. In some ways, the chief financial officer's role in a strategy-focused organization is more difficult than that of the chief executive. To be optimistic, show leadership, and advocate change is a natural, almost stereotypical role for the chief executive. The chief financial officer, however, is likely expected to have a conservative mien: to safeguard the money, prudently invest the endowment for the long-term, resist excessive spending, and continually remind everyone of the costs of the plans that emerge from the process. Yet the chief financial officer should avoid acting too cautiously lest he or she become a roadblock to progress. Accurate data and truthful opinions are still essential to the role of the chief financial officer, but so is an outlook that will enable the process to succeed.[5]

How can adequate resources be mobilized? What are the most realistic forecasts of revenues, expenses, and endowment returns? A chief financial officer can be most effective by doing the following:

· Establishing the institutional research and cost capability to support planning and budgeting.

· Developing financial planning models that link with the strategic plan.

· Providing analyses that reveal the impact of various assumptions on the strategic and financial plans.

---

[5] Kent John Chabotar, "Business Managers and Academic Officers: Making the Relationship Work," *Business Officer* (September 1989), pp. 38-40.

- Providing staff support to various board committees for development of the financial plan and budget, investment policy, performance measurement, due diligence, investment accounting, and analysis.

- Developing relationships with commercial bankers, business leaders, and legislators as the need arises.

- Promoting inclusion of the major maintenance program and campus master plan into the planning and budgeting processes.

- Offering alternative funding scenarios that include operating budget revenues as well as capital gifts, debt, quasi-endowment funds, special state appropriations, and budget reallocations.

- Maintaining objectivity and forthrightness in meetings while also enthusiastically supporting the chief executive and the planning process.

Chief Academic Officer. The chief academic officer has a major role in planning and budgeting. The academic program constitutes the institution's "core business," which is the centerpiece of any meaningful strategic plan. About one-half of the budget usually is devoted to instruction and academic support (the library and instructional computing, for example). In large institutions, the chief academic officer also is the provost and has overall responsibility for developing the annual budget and long-range financial plan.

A partnership between the chief academic officer and the chief financial officer is essential to driving change at any institution. The chief financial officer helps provide the data the chief academic officer needs to support existing programs and new initiatives. The chief academic officer, in turn, serves as a bridge to the faculty for the chief financial officer in explaining the financial constraints on planning and budgeting.

The chief academic officer participates effectively by doing the following:

- Advocating for academic programs while being sensitive to larger institutional issues and priorities.

- Working with faculty to develop criteria and standards for adding and deleting academic programs in advance of any crisis.

- Requiring reliable revenue and cost data for any new programs or initiatives.

- Aligning faculty hiring with the strategic plan in terms of numbers and assignments.

- Developing transparent methods for allocating budgets among departments by numbers of majors, contact hours, or other factors related to workload.

- Working with the chief financial officer to ensure that ratios in the academic program (the number of full-time faculty or the student-faculty ratio, for example) and elsewhere adhere to the strategic plan and contribute to reaffirmation of accreditation.

Other Senior Officers. Three other senior administrators have significant responsibilities in the planning process — the chief admissions, development, and student affairs officers.

The chief admissions officer is prominent because enrollment and financial-aid levels are influential budget drivers. Strategic plans may be impaired if applications, acceptances, or yield drop below targets or if the yield contains a disproportionately high number of students who need large amounts of aid or a low number who can pay full tuition.

The chief development officer oversees the annual and capital giving efforts that support the plan and budget. For both the chief admissions and development officers, it is critical not to make unrealistic financial promises despite pressures for a funded plan or balanced budget.

Finally, the chief student affairs officer speaks to the co-curricular and extracurricular aspects of the institution as reflected in the strategic plan and budget. This individual must work closely with the chief academic and admissions officers because enrollment depends not only on new admissions but also on retention of present students. In turn, retention is affected mightily by faculty-student interactions, class sizes, and the overall quality of the academic program. Retention rates also depend on the quality of extracurricular activities, dining services, and the residence program for which the chief student affairs officer is responsible.

Faculty, Staff, and Students. Representatives of these groups often sit on board committees and may even serve as voting members of the full board of trustees. These individuals are affiliated with units that make strategic, programmatic, and financial proposals. For example, if there is a student government budget, students may be involved in preparing student services and athletics budgets. In fact, if the campus planning and budgeting processes truly are participatory, students may be part of the governance apparatus that develops and approves the strategy, plans, and budget.

Faculty, staff, and students, too, can be important sources of information on the academic program, competition in the marketplace, and support for the institution's mission, goals, and core values.

Proposals for major change, no matter how strategically justified, will usually be resisted when vital interests are threatened. What Gordon Winston wrote in 1993 still rings true today: "The fundamental challenge to college administrators over the next few years, arguably, will be to induce a highly resistant community to understand that there's an economic reality within which they'll have to live, one that may include 'downsizing' and 'restructuring' and the biting of all sorts of painful bullets."[6]

Alumni. In addition to being a major source of financial support, alumni are the living memory of the institution. They often become involved in setting the strategy and in environmental and marketplace assessment. Young alumni also can help assess the relevance of the curriculum. A strategy-focused organization should take into account that alumni may resist institutional change, seeking to freeze the institution in the form and time of their personal experience.

---

[6] Gordon Winston, "New Dangers in Old Traditions: The Reporting of Economic Performance in Colleges and Universities," *Change* (January/February, 1993), p. 25.

Legal Counsel. Staff attorneys assist in strategic planning by performing due diligence on assumptions and action steps in the plan, such as the impact on the college charter, guidelines for terminating staff and programs, and entry into new markets and services. They also may provide legal reviews for the issuance of bonds and interpret bylaws and state statutes that both empower and limit administrative and even governing board discretion. Legal counsel is less successfully employed in evaluating the substance of strategic and financial choices having to do with the institutional mission and budget allocations.

Consultants. Besides offering the option of flexible staffing, consultants often bring special expertise and credibility to the strategic planning process. Prevalent uses of consultants include the following:

· Assessing needs in admissions and financial aid, information technology, facilities and space use, compensation and benefits, and other assumptions underlying the strategic and financial plans.

· Providing historical and comparative data about investment performance and identifying potential opportunities.

· Gathering internal information directly from faculty, staff, and students on strategic direction, budget allocations, leadership, and other matters.

· Improving decision-making processes that support strategic planning, budgeting, and management of administrative and clerical staff.

In the 1990s, Bowdoin College used consultants in peer reviews in a process that was similar to a decennial reaccreditation. A peer-review committee was formed of three or more members from comparable institutions and the professional association for that department. For example, when the physical plant department was studied, Bowdoin selected expert reviewers from Colby College, Education Development Center Inc., and the American Physical Plant Association. An on-campus committee was selected that represented key constituencies to draft review questions and to host the review committee. After several days of data collection, analysis, and interviews of departmental staff and customers, peer reviewers were orally debriefed by the on-campus committee, which subsequently submitted a written report to the board. Besides the physical plant, the peer-review committee was used to assist management in assessing the bookstore, computing and information services, and campus security.

Government officials. Because the governor and state legislators approve funding for public institutions' strategic plans, institutional leaders at both the system and campus levels must keep them informed throughout the process. Public officials in state education agencies and bonding authorities also become involved as sources for assumptions cited in the strategic and financial plans.

Every college and university has a budget. Many have some sense of direction or strategy if not a formal strategic plan. But few link the budget to the strategic plan, and thus fail to make strategic decisions in the context of current and projected financial resources. Without this linkage, finances are used almost solely to prevent spending rather than as a source of needed investments in strategy or human and physical resources. A strategy-focused organization centers its finances and other components on its mission and goals. It fully realizes the costs of major goals and priorities and thus promotes benchmarking and market comparisons. The strategic plan creates the long-range financial plan, which, in turn, frames the annual budget.

CHAPTER 3

Strategic Planning: Contexts and Ends

S trategic planning, succinctly defined, is a "disciplined effort to produce fundamental decisions and actions that shape and guide what an organization is, what it does, and why it does it."[1] Typically extending five to seven years, the strategic plan sets basic directions for the organization that will help differentiate it from competitors in terms of quality, cost, and other attributes. The plan comprises a mission, goals and objectives, the programs and policies needed to attain them, and the people and offices responsible for the plan's execution. It flows from both prior plans and current needs, as well as from an honest assessment of environmental allies, adversaries, and the competitive market in which the college or university operates.

A strategic plan is a means of setting priorities that in turn are tied to reality by action steps and financing. Through the highlighting of their special strengths, colleges and universities may achieve a sustainable competitive advantage over rivals. A strategic plan is *not* a program-by-program blueprint or a schematic drawing that details every implementation step.

In this chapter, strategic planning is explored via the concept of "competitive advantage" and five basic steps of the planning process. The discussion focuses on knowing the organizational context of planning (Steps 1 and 2) and the identification of the organizational ends that planning aims to define (Steps 3 to 5). These ends include mission, core values, goals, and objectives that are described in increasing levels of specificity. These must be established before the means and evaluation — the topics of Chapter 4 — can take place.

Not all plans are strategic. Operational plans are more specific than strategic plans, have shorter terms (three years or less), and contain "how to" statements for specific projects or departments. Human-resources plans deal with the long-range staffing needs of the institution, recruitment areas and strategies, and succession planning (for example, people identified as on the "fast track" to promotion or viewed as prime internal candidates for senior positions). Long-range financial and contingency plans are folded into other parts of the strategic plan, though they are deemed separate at some institutions.

Harvard Business School Professor Michael Porter postulates a useful approach to strategic planning.[2] He defines "competitive advantage" as the ability to utilize the organization's distinctive competencies to create superior value for its customers. This value is produced by delivering either the same product at lower cost (cost

---

[1] John M. Bryson, *Strategic Planning for Public and Nonprofit Organizations: A Guide to Strengthening and Sustaining Organizational Achievement* (San Francisco: Jossey-Bass, 1995). See also: H. Mintzberg, "The Fall and Rise of Strategic Planning," *Harvard Business Review* (January/February 1994), pp. 107-114; University of North Carolina at Greensboro, *The UNCG Plan 1998*; Ohio State University, *Academic Plan* (October 2000); Roosevelt University, *Strategic Plan* (April 1998).

[2] Michael E. Porter, *Competitive Advantage* (New York: Free Press, 1998).

advantage) or a better product at the same cost (differentiation advantage). A simple long-range plan would not be that ambitious. Guilford College's plan, for example, adopted a comprehensive set of initiatives to secure its competitive advantage:

> Our strategy to gain competitive advantage involves both preservation and change. [Guilford College] aims to preserve its special character as an undergraduate liberal arts college guided by Quaker testimonies that emphasize creative and critical thinking and service learning with small classes and superb teaching. We seek not only to preserve but also to improve an unusual academic program where all students sample the liberal arts and pre-professional programs and benefit from a diverse population of students.
>
> Dramatic change will be manifested by a new curricular focus on principled problem solving and the documented integration of academic courses with service, work experience, and a skill-based co-curriculum — a focus that reflects our Quaker practices and emphasis on all things "civil and useful." Change will also be demonstrated by leveraging all of the above to increase enrollment by 32 percent to 3,300 students — ranging in age from 16 to 60 — an increase that will make us more cost-efficient and that will provide revenues needed to develop a larger, better paid faculty to strengthen the curriculum, improve facilities, and secure other attributes of educational excellence.[3]

Dwight D. Eisenhower was once quoted as saying, "In preparing for battle I have always found that plans are useless, but planning is indispensable."[4] Some varieties of process models are detailed below:

- During the 1990s, the president of the State University of New York at Farmingdale achieved his vision that the institution would be transformed from a two-year, general purpose technical college to a four-year baccalaureate institution. It was clearly a presidential, "top down" plan.[5]

- By contrast, planning at the New York Botanical Garden was a widely participative, "bottom up" process in which each division explained its view of the future to everyone else. Eventually, the views were amalgamated into a single planning document accompanied by a capital campaign and a separate facilities plan.[6]

- Guilford College represents a third model. A planning group consisting of senior officers, faculty, students, and administrative and support staff was divided into subcommittees that interacted with one another and with the larger academic community throughout a two-year process. During the first year, the subcommittees

---

[3] "Strategic Plan for Guilford College: Creative Leadership for the 21ˢᵗ Century," (May 2005), p. 43.

[4] Richard M. Nixon, "Khrushchev," *Six Crises* (Garden City, N.Y.: Doubleday, 1962).

[5] James P. Honan, *et al. SUNY College of Technology at Farmingdale*, Case Study (Cambridge, Mass.: Harvard Graduate School of Education, 1997).

[6] Jeanne M. Liedtka, *Strategic Planning at the New York Botanical Garden*, Case Study (Charlottesville, Va.: University of Virginia, Darden Business School, 1997).

focused on external assessment, internal analysis, and core values. Subcommittees were reconfigured in the second year to focus on content development outlined in the plan: transformational education, leadership and social impact, community, and stewardship.

In each of the above cases, financial exigencies inspired the planning effort with a new vision in order to focus scarce resources and raise money. For example, state budget problems affected almost the entire SUNY system. Farmingdale's president viewed the change in mission as crucial to improving the institution's image, attracting students, and gaining public support. A fiscal crisis in New York City not only spurred the planning effort but also prompted the Botanical Garden to emphasize revenue generation in the plan, including charging admission fees for the first time. At Guilford College, one reason the budget chronically was unbalanced was the need to fund an academic program that included 80 undergraduate majors and concentrations but only 1,500 students. The planning effort led to a decision to increase enrollment to 3,300 students in five years and to establish criteria for program elimination and new program approval.

A second key factor in these three cases was the decision to broaden the involvement of the governing board in each case beyond merely approving the final draft of the plan. The trustees at Guilford made developing a strategic plan part of the mandate of the new president and established a planning committee to work alongside the campus planning committee by providing advice and informally encouraging bold thinking. At the Botanical Garden, trustees not only were briefed on how planning was progressing, but they also served on the committee that developed the plan. The chief executive invited an economist to a board retreat to talk about the economic effects on private philanthropy. He also insisted on linking specific budget requests to the long-term vision embedded in the strategic plan. The president of SUNY Farmingdale involved the board at many stages that included approving a fundamental change in mission from an essentially lower division institution to a specialized four-year college of technology — eliminating and adding programs based on the new mission — and responding with program proposals such as an academic industrial park when trustees asked for revenue-producing projects tied to the mission.

Elements of a Strategic Plan

Strategic plans come in many shapes and sizes. If approaches to planning were placed along a continuum, at one extreme would be incremental planning, an approach that makes modest changes to the status quo to address a specific issue such as a new quadrangle, enrollment growth, or faculty size. At the other extreme of the continuum would lie comprehensive planning. This approach essentially asks planners to rebuild the organization from a zero base and encourages "blue sky" thinking. Both extremes, and gradations in between, involve a logical sequence of steps of increasing specificity as shown in Exhibit 3.0.

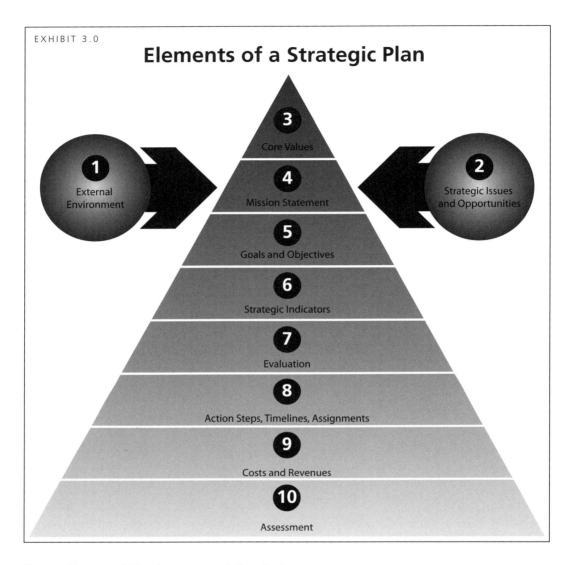

EXHIBIT 3.0

Elements of a Strategic Plan

1 External Environment

2 Strategic Issues and Opportunities

3 Core Values

4 Mission Statement

5 Goals and Objectives

6 Strategic Indicators

7 Evaluation

8 Action Steps, Timelines, Assignments

9 Costs and Revenues

10 Assessment

Step 1: External Environmental Analysis

An environmental scan and analysis defines the immediate and general operating environment of the institution. This process sets the context for and constraints on the strategic plan. Following are some of the issues an environmental analysis addresses:

· New developments in curricular content and pedagogy such as new curriculum concentrations and ways of teaching and learning.

· Trends in student demographics in terms of ethnic and racial groups, international origin, gender, and socioeconomic groups, all or some of which might have a significant impact on enrollments, revenues, financial aid, facilities, and programs.

· Student demand — what do students want? Institutions often focus on what *they* want to do instead of determining if there is an actual or potential market for a new program or major.

- Economic trends that affect price inflation, affordability of tuition, ability to pay, faculty and staff job markets, employment opportunities for students and graduates, and the availability of private and government support.

- Status of current and emerging competitors that includes not only other traditional colleges and universities but also proprietary institutions and corporate training programs;

- Changes in federal or state policies such as funding priorities, safety and security regulations, and accountability procedures;

- Increasing globalization of education, as exemplified by the technological revolution in information and communications, exchange programs, and emphasis on international business and related fields in the curriculum; and

- Shifts in accreditation standards that may affect decisions about curriculum, finances and facilities, assessment, and other functions of the institution.

Step 2: Strategic Issues and Opportunities

Driven in part by the environmental analysis, but also by the institution's own history and capabilities, strategic issues and opportunities suggest the vital areas for which the strategic plan must set direction. These areas may include the following:

- Curriculum, programs, and majors;

- Academic reputation — especially when actual and perceived reputations are different;

- Admissions and retention;

- Faculty recruitment and retirement;

- Student life, including athletics;

- Finances, including budgeting and fund-raising;

- Facilities, including the appearance and functionality of new construction and major renovations as well as current and deferred maintenance;

- Academic and administrative technology systems, software, and equipment; and

- Community relations with governments, including those with civic and voluntary organizations, news media, and the citizenry.

In its annual higher education outlook, Moody's Investors Services noted the following opportunities and challenges of higher education with special relevance to finances, as shown in Exhibit 3.1.[7]

---

[7] Moody's Investors Service, *2005 Higher Education Outlook: Stable Outlook for Both Public and Private Institutions* (March 2005).

Exhibit 3.1: Strengths and Challenges in Higher Education

	Strengths	Challenges
Private Colleges and Universities	Stronger economy, investment markets, and demographics in most markets supporting healthy tuition pricing.	Competition from public institutions, cuts in governmental financial aid, and weakening demographics in some parts of the country.
	Improved investment returns, which have fueled philanthropy and endowment returns.	Asset allocations moving toward alternative investments, which require greater oversight.
	Historically low interest rates that make debt more affordable.	Pressure to invest in capital facilities leading to debt growth.
	Stronger focus on financial management including more conservative budgeting.	Aggressive plans for growth in research despite slow growth of federal research budget.
Public Colleges and Universities	Student demand remains sound, driven by low tuition (compared with private institutions) and solid demographic trends.	Demographics peaking in some regions.
	Many institutions retain pricing flexibility.	Continued revenue pressure with flat state funding and political pressure to limit tuition increases.
	Overall positive operating performance despite tight state spending environment.	Investment in facilities to accommodate growing enrollment, increase research space, and attract competitive student body.
	Financial pressure retention or growth.	Policy issues about the role of public higher education; tensions between institutional autonomy and increased state oversight.

Step 3: Core Values

Core values are the essential — and enduring — tenets of the organization, independent of shifts in educational or societal values and current challenges and opportunities. [8] For example, if higher education in ten years does not care about social justice, will your institution still have social justice on its list of core values? Core values are not developed so much as *identified*; they need only be discovered and defined. Corporations, too, have espoused core values, some examples of which are well known:

· Nordstrom values service to the customer above all else, hard work and individual productivity, never being satisfied, excellence in reputation, and being part of something special.

· Sony values elevation of the Japanese culture and national status, being a pioneer and not following others, doing the impossible, and encouraging individual ability and creativity.

· Walt Disney Company nurtures and promulgates wholesome American values, creativity, dreams, and imagination; fanatical attention to consistency and detail; and preservation and control of the "Disney magic."[9]

---

[8] James C. Collins and Jerry I. Porras, "Building Your Company's Vision," *Harvard Business Review* (September/October 1996), pp. 65-77.

[9] "Core Values," *www.engin.umd.umich.edu/CIS/strat.plan/values.htm.* (accessed August 24, 2006.)

In higher education, core values tend to be more numerous and less concise. This is often because of the need to add certain words that appeal to specific constituencies in order to achieve consensus. Exhibit 3.2 contains a sampling of such core values.[10]

Exhibit 3.2: Sample Core Values

Institution	Core Value	Definition
University of Texas at Austin	Learning	A caring community, all of us students, helping one another grow.
	Discovery	Expanding knowledge and human understanding.
	Freedom	To seek the truth and express it.
	Leadership	The will to excel with integrity and the spirit that nothing is impossible.
	Individual Opportunity	Many options, diverse people and ideas; one university.
	Responsibility	To serve as a catalyst for positive change in Texas and beyond.
University of Pennsylvania Health System	Excellence	We will strive for excellence through creativity and innovation.
	Integrity	We will be truthful, equitable and committed to intellectual honesty.
	Diversity	We will foster intellectual, racial, social and cultural diversity.
	Professionalism	We will achieve the highest standards of professionalism through ethical behavior, collaboration, self-education and respect for all members of UPHS.
	Individual Opportunity	We support equal opportunity and individual creativity and innovation.
	Teamwork and Collaboration	We will support each other and promote collaboration with our colleagues and thoughtful stewardship of university and UPHS resources.
	Tradition	We will learn from our history, take responsibility for the future and promote the unique nature of the Penn environment.
Joliet Junior College	Respect	The community advocates respect for every individual by the demonstration of courtesy and civility in every endeavor.
	Integrity	Integrity is an integral component of the common bond among community members.
	Collaboration	Joliet Junior College is dedicated to the formation and enrichment of collaborative relationships as part of the scholarly process.
	Humor and Well Being	The staff recognizes humor as a means for collegial well-being and self-rejuvenation.
	Innovation	Encouraging the pursuit of excellence and innovation drives Joliet Junior College through the 21st century.
	Quality	Joliet Junior College is dedicated to the quality of its educational programs and services.

---

[10] University of Texas at Austin, "Mission," *www.utexas.edu/welcome/mission.html, www.uphs.upenn.edu/about_uphs/values.html, www.jjc.edu/main/core_value.htm* (accessed August 6, 2006.)

Step 4: Mission

As the fundamental statement of purpose, the mission states the organization's reason for existing. It is the substantive and philosophical source for the strategic plan. It should reflect a central theme and identify the most important attributes of the institution. Corporations often get this right, such as: "Give ordinary folks the chance to buy the same thing as rich people" (Wal Mart) and "Make people happy" (Walt Disney).

Mission statements for higher education generally are longer, but they still should be limited to a few sentences. Although brief, the mission is often difficult to develop. All campus constituencies know that the mission is the basis for the plan and want to see their interests and programs reflected in the mission, if only by a single word.

A few examples show how lofty and inspirational the mission can be:

- The Mission of Saint Louis University is the pursuit of truth for the greater glory of God and for the service of humanity. The university seeks excellence in the fulfillment of its corporate purposes of teaching, research, and community service. It is dedicated to leadership in the continuing quest for understanding of God's creation and for the discovery, dissemination, and integration of the values, knowledge, and skills required to transform society in the spirit of the Gospels. As a Catholic, Jesuit university, the pursuit is motivated by the inspiration and values of the Judeo-Christian tradition and is guided by the spiritual and intellectual ideals of the Society of Jesus.

- Manchester College respects the infinite worth of every individual and graduates persons of ability and conviction who draw upon their education and faith to lead principled, productive, and compassionate lives that improve the human condition.

- The mission of the system is to develop human resources, to discover and disseminate knowledge, to extend knowledge and its application beyond the boundaries of its campuses, and to serve and stimulate society by developing in students heightened intellectual, cultural, and humane sensitivities, scientific, professional, and technological expertise, and a sense of purpose. Inherent in this broad mission are methods of instruction, research, extended training, and public service designed to educate people and improve the human condition. Basic to every purpose of the system is the search for truth. (University of Wisconsin)

Colleges and universities tend to develop missions that describe what they *are* instead of what *they want to become*. In other words, the mission often reflects the status quo in order to justify it. A college may have a curricular focus on undergraduate liberal arts and, without much consideration of alternatives or data, write the mission to stay that way. An effective mission does not have to evoke major change, but it should result from systematic collection and analysis of data, consideration of core values and alternatives, and community participation. After lengthy study and debate, an undergraduate liberal arts college might properly recommit the mission to the same focus, or it might add business or graduate education to its mission.

"Mission creep" is a second challenge. A term that was first applied to military operations, mission creep is the expansion of the mission beyond its original intent

— a common phenomenon occurring after early successes or in pursuit of funding opportunities. For example, an undergraduate college might add an engineering school because of a $25 million gift or continue to add majors and programs to attract new students. Such extensions dilute the power and focus of the mission and may lead to overextension and loss of financial equilibrium.

Step 5: Goals and Objectives

The mission becomes more concrete by being subdivided into related general goals; these goals are then further broken down into more specific objectives. Often, planners attach "vision" statements that describe what the institution will be like if the goals and objectives are achieved.

Called by differing names, "goals" are broad statements of strategic intent that describe what the organization will be like or how it will change if the mission is achieved. Some organizations label their goals "strategic objectives," while others use the term "continuing objective." A mission might have five or more goals (but seldom more than ten) in order to focus attention and resources on the organization's most important aims, as stressed by another synonym for goal, "strategic priority."

Some argue that successful organizations keep core values intact while articulating audacious goals and programs in order to adapt to a changing world. This calls for "such a big commitment that when people see what the goal will take, there's almost an audible gasp."[11]

By this reasoning, colleges and universities can aim for the top tier of the *U.S. News & World Report* rankings, double their enrollment, or radically alter their curriculum — while remaining true to their core values. With such a strategy, they may define their goals ambitiously, envision what the institution will be like if they accomplish the goals, and then mobilize resources and programs to that end.

Exhibit 3.3 compares the goals of Ohio State University and the University of Kentucky (as identified by West Virginia University as part of its own strategic planning process).

Exhibit 3.3: Sample Goals

Goals: Ohio State University	Goals: University of Kentucky
Build a World-Class Faculty	Reach for National Prominence
Develop Academic Programs that Define Ohio State as the Nation's Leading Public Land-Grant University	Attract and Graduate Outstanding Students
Improve the Quality of the Teaching and Learning Environment	Attract, Develop and Retain a Distinguished Faculty
Enhance and Better Serve the Student Body	Discover, Share and Apply New Knowledge
Create a More Diverse University Community	Nurture Diversity of Thought, Culture, Gender and Ethnicity
Help Build Ohio's Future	Elevate the Quality of Life for Kentuckians

[11] Collins and Porras, pp. 65-77.

In contrast to goals, objectives are specific outcomes to be achieved within a definite time, usually a year or two, related to the accomplishment of one or more goals. While the terms often are used interchangeably, the inclusion of deadlines and specific outcomes is the hallmark of this level of the plan. Not all objectives have individual deadlines. If the strategic plan covers, for example, 2005-10, it is assumed without contrary evidence that the objectives are due for 2010. As the most concrete expressions of the "ends" of the plan, objectives serve as the basis for defining the "means" or specific action steps. They also are essential to the assessment of organizational effectiveness to the extent they are concrete and measurable, either directly or by linking to strategic indicators. A goal may have only one objective in order to focus attention and increase the chances of success, or it may have many if needs are immense or resources abundant.

Below is a sampling of goals and objectives with varying levels of specificity and use of deadlines:

Michigan State University, College of Social Science.

Goal 1 — Mission-Oriented: Identify and develop outstanding signature programs.

Vision 2007 — Signature programs are established as long-term academic activity that reflect our unique identity as a college. Signature programs showcase our national and international areas of excellence.

Objectives — Every unit in the college is associated with at least one signature program. Plans are implemented to advance the quality and standing of all disciplines, schools, and programs in the college.

Ball State University

Goal 1: Ball State University will enhance excellence in undergraduate and graduate learning.

1. Prepare graduates who demonstrate achievement in the knowledge, skills, and values that are expected by the university and developed through experiences in and out of the classroom.

2. Support and create outstanding undergraduate programs, including the university core curriculum and the honors college.

3. Strengthen Ball State's commitment to graduate education by increasing support for outstanding programs and faculty scholarship.

4. Set high expectations for student academic achievement, personal responsibility, and campus involvement and frequently recognize student success.

5. Provide all students with enhanced learning opportunities through international, internship, research, service learning, and leadership development experiences.

6. Use strong program review and assessment evidence to improve the quality of instructional resources, academic programs, and student learning and development.

7. Integrate learning with faculty scholarship consistent with the teacher-scholar model.

8. Support a collegial environment that encourages faculty and professional personnel to interact with each other and with students.

Guilford College

Strategic Priority 1-1: Emphasize principled problem solving as a distinctive and central theme of academic programs at Guilford College.

Vision: In 2010, Guilford College has a national reputation for practical liberal arts education that contributes to the life and health of local, national, and global communities in a concrete fashion. Employers in search of problem solvers hire Guilford College alumni. Graduate programs that seek to attract creative and critical thinkers who integrate theory and practice recruit at Guilford College. Community organizations and businesses that struggle to resolve vexing problems come to Guilford for creative solutions.

Objective 1: By 2007, Guilford College will create a Center for Principled Problem Solving.

Objective 2: By 2007, in conjunction with its reaccreditation and ongoing assessment, Guilford College will implement revisions to years one and two of the general education curriculum by introducing students to interdisciplinary approaches to complex problems and preparing them to analyze complex problems, and to help them achieve a high level of competence in reading, writing, quantitative reasoning, and creative and critical thinking.

Objective 3: By 2009, Guilford College will identify academic outcomes reflecting effective foundational preparation in reading, writing, quantitative reasoning, and creative and critical thinking across the curriculum, as well as identifying faculty competent in analyzing complex systems necessary to engagement with problem solving.

Examining the environmental challenges and strategic issues that confront institutions is an exciting enterprise. It places the college and community in the "real world" of economics, politics, demographics, technology, and other forces. How the institution chooses to respond in the long term is indicated by identifying the mission and vision and core values to guide the effort. General goals and more specific objectives can then be framed for the limited period covered by the strategic plan. This is the essence of strategic thinking. At this point, the college or university has completed the "ends" and can proceed to detail the means and resources needed to accomplish those ends.

CHAPTER 4

Strategic Planning: Evaluation and Means

Evaluating strategic planning efforts consists of at least two steps: first, identifying the specific strategic indicators that effectively will measure how well the institution is accomplishing its stated objectives, and second, assessing whether the plan is on time and on budget. The means to strategic planning are the action steps needed to connect the plan to reality and to specify the needed human, physical, and financial resources to ensure its acceptance.

This chapter focuses on the remaining "Action Steps" — numbers six through ten — that cover the strategic indicators and processes needed to effectively connect the substance and process of planning to obtain buy-in and support from major stakeholders and constituencies.

Step 6: Strategic Indicators

Most objectives require a set of strategic indicators to measure progress toward achievement. A strategic indicator measures organizational performance in a critical decision area and is used to shape, inform, and support policymaking. It connects planning and action, provides concrete targets around which to mobilize enthusiasm and resources, improves accountability for results, and promotes the use of data for decision making.

Not all indicators are strategic. Strategic indicators are, by definition, connected to a strategic plan or at least strategic thinking in a specific area. An institution can still use indicators to monitor trends but without the sense of direction and priority that a plan bestows. One common use of these "other" indicators occurs in the financial area, where colleges and universities routinely compile data on budget performance, endowment size, student fees, and other measures. Unless these indicators are linked to the plan, they are not really strategic. In such cases, however, financial indicators may trigger a strategic planning process — especially if the trends are negative.

Strategic and other indicators advance benchmarking by using industry standards or competitors' data to compare and evaluate key programs and services. Colby–Sawyer College in New Hampshire, for example, categorized its 28 strategic indicators into three broad goals: quality of the learning community, financial strength, and niche.[1] Some of the most salient indicators often relate to efficiency and productivity, financial outcomes, student and educational outcomes, and rankings such as those published by *U.S. News & World Report*.

Efficiency and Productivity. Efficiency and productivity can be ends in themselves — especially in an institution undergoing retrenchment or administrative reform — or they can be strategic indicators that measure how much input is required to achieve objectives. Objectives frequently are correlated with staffing and workload statistics. For example, the college may study the relationship between an academic department's budget and its enrollment, average class size, student-faculty ratio, and teaching load.

---

[1] Anne Ponder, "A Four-Page Strategic Plan," *Trusteeship* (March/April 2000), pp. 20-23.

Financial Outcomes. Other indicators detect whether the budget supports its vision and priorities without necessarily evaluating results. For example:

- The share of total revenue supplied by student fees evidences *affordability* and how financial-aid policies affect net revenue.

- Trends in revenue earned from government appropriations and annual giving suggest *external support*.

- Government and foundation-sponsored programs imply the centrality of *research*.

- The proportion of the budget spent on instruction and academic support, such as libraries and information technology, suggests the importance of *teaching*.

- Expenses for student services and auxiliary enterprises, such as food service and dormitories, suggest the quality of *student life*.

- Expenses incurred for operation and maintenance of plant as well as new construction and other capital projects reveal priorities with regard to the preservation of *physical assets*.

- Expenses for employee training, tuition reimbursement, and faculty and staff compensation can indicate *preservation of human assets*.

Student Learning Outcomes. The most concrete measures used for student learning outcomes are student retention, graduation, and employment rates, passing grades on exams such as teacher certification tests or GREs, and admission to graduate school.

Ideally, colleges and universities should correlate budgets with gains in instruction, research, and service. Measurement seems easier for scholarly activity (for example, the number of grant applications funded or scholarly works published) than for student learning. In their efforts to justify the costs of a course or degree program, most institutions are unable to point to measurable outcomes. Trustees from the corporate world, accustomed to stringent market and profitability tests for products and services, often are mystified by this inability.

The situation is changing, however. The definition and assessment of student learning outcomes is an increasingly important focus of accreditation. For example, the Higher Learning Commission of the North Central Association — the largest postsecondary accreditation association in the U.S. — mandates learning outcomes as one of its core components: "The organization's goals for student learning outcomes are clearly stated for each educational program and make effective assessment possible."[2] Among the evidence that the North Central Association suggests to show compliance with the core component are that the institution (1) clearly differentiates its learning outcomes for undergraduate, graduate, and post-baccalaureate programs by identifying the expected learning outcomes for each; and (2) promotes assessment of learning outcomes at multiple levels: course, program, and institutional.[3]

---

[2] The Higher Learning Commission, *Handbook of Accreditation* (Chicago: North Central Association, 2003) pp. 3.2-9.

[3] *Ibid.*

The Southern Association of Colleges and Schools (SACS) also emphasizes student learning outcomes in its core requirement for a "Quality Enhancement Plan." The QEP is based on a "comprehensive and thorough analysis of the effectiveness of the learning environment for supporting student learning and accomplishing the mission of the institution." The criteria for an acceptable QEP echo many of the themes of this book, as they include adequate resources in place to implement the plan and evidence of community development and support of the plan.[4]

U.S. News & World Report Rankings. There are many sets of strategic indicators reflected in the annual rankings of colleges and universities published by *U.S. News & World Report*. Rankings are based on seven broad areas, each with specific factors that constitute strategic indicators. The weights for each category for national doctoral universities and liberal arts colleges are shown in Exhibit 4.0.[5]

Exhibit 4.0: Weights For Rankings In *U.S. News & World Report*

Ranking Category	Weight — National Doctoral and Liberal Arts Institutions	Sub factors
1. Academic reputation	25%	Academic reputation survey
2. Student selectivity	15%	Acceptance rate
		Yield
		High school class standing
		SAT/ACT scores
3. Faculty resources	20%	Faculty compensation
		% faculty terminal degree
		% full-time faculty
		Student-faculty ratio
		Class size, 1-19 students
		Class size, 50+ students
4. Graduation/retention	20%	Average graduation rate
		Average freshman
		Retention
5. Financial resources	10%	Average educational expenditures per student
6. Alumni giving	5%	Average giving rate
7. Graduation rate performance	5%	Graduation rate

---

[4] Commission on Colleges, *Resource Manual for the Principles of Accreditation* (Decatur, Ga.: Southern Association of Colleges and Schools, 2005) pp. 21-22.

[5] Daniel J. Levin, *The Uses and Abuses of the U.S. News Rankings* (Washington, D.C.: Association of Governing Boards of Universities and Colleges: Fall 2002), p.3. See also: *www.usnews.com/usnews/edu/college/rankings/about/weight_brief.php*

Thomas Corts and James Eck in their *Trusteeship* article, "Ten Ways to Track Performance," recommend that trustees watch the following "institutional vitality indicators":

- Total expendable financial resources per FTE student *(total net assets, minus net investments in plant, divided by full-time equivalent student)*. Moody's Investors Services states that this indicator of financial strength and institutional perpetuity has the highest correlation to default of all its ratios.

- Expendable financial resources to debt *(total unrestricted net assets, plus temporarily restricted net assets, minus investment in plant, divided by outstanding debt)*. This ratio measures the ability of the college or university to access funds to reduce debt.

- Expendable financial resources to operations *(total unrestricted net assets, plus temporarily restricted net assets, minus net investment in plant, divided by total expenditures)*. This ratio measures how many years the institution could survive solely by using reserves.

- Average peak debt-service coverage *(three-year average operating surplus, plus interest expense, plus depreciation expense, divided by maximum annual debt service)*. What is the extent to which annual operations ensure the ability to cover existing debt?

- Applicants to admits *(selectivity and matriculation ratios)*. This indicator is a measure of admissions selectivity that can fluctuate to increase enrollment or improve quality.

- Tuition rate changes *(tracked over five years)*. This ratio is a measure of pricing flexibility and the capacity of the institution to raise additional revenue by tuition increases.

- Enrollment levels *(tracked over five years)*. Since student fees often are the largest single source of revenue, the number of students is a crucial indicator of institutional health.

- Retention rate *(from freshman to sophomore years)*. A low retention rate is a sign of poor fit between student needs and expectations and the institution's culture and offerings. A low rate adds additional pressure and cost for replacement of students lost.

- Graduation rates *(four-year, five-year, and six-year rates)*. Graduation rates are retention rates spread over selected time periods and are widely perceived by the public to be indicators of institutional attractiveness and quality.

- Instructional expenditures per FTE student. This indicator measures the extent to which the college or university is funding what may be called its "core business."[6]

Composite Financial Index. The Composite Financial Index (CFI) was developed by KPMG and Prager, Sealy & Co., LLC, for use in financial benchmarking in higher education.[7] It is designed to provide a more comprehensive assessment of financial health than is possible by simply comparing multiple ratios or indicators. The CFI is based on four ratios:

---

[6] Thomas E. Corts and James C. Eck, "Ten Ways to Track Performance," *Trusteeship* (January/February 2002), pp. 14-18.

[7] F.J. Prager et al., *Strategic Financial Analysis for Higher Education*, 6th ed (Prager, Sealy, & Co., LLC, KPMG LLP, and BearingPoint Inc., 2005). See also: The Austen Group, *Financial Indicators Tool* (Washington, D.C.: Council of Independent Colleges, 2005); and M.K. Townsley, *The Small College Guide to Financial Health: Beating the Odds* (Washington, D.C.: National Association of College and University Business Officers, 2002).

1. *Primary Reserve Ratio.* The primary reserve ratio measures the financial reserves that the institution could use if needed to meet unexpected opportunities or a budget crisis. It divides expendable net assets by total expenses. In other words, the total resources that the college or university could spend on operations are divided by the total expenses for the year.[8] In 2005, the University of North Carolina at Chapel Hill (UNC-CH) had expendable net assets of $1.2 billion which when divided by total expenses of $1.7 billion yielded a ratio of 0.71.[9] The target is at least 0.40, which means, among other things, that the institution could survive for about 40 percent of the year, or five months, with no additional revenue. A ratio below 0.15 usually means that the institution must use short-term borrowing to cover operating expenses. This ratio constitutes 35 percent of the CFI.

2. *Net Income Ratio.* This ratio assesses whether student fees and other revenues earned from day-to-day operations are sufficient to cover salaries, depreciation, and other expenses. Is the institution living within available resources? Budget surpluses create opportunities for new investments in plant and programs as long as exorbitant student fees, overspending from endowment, or underspending on mission-critical activities do not eat them up. Chronic large budget deficits sap an institution's financial strength by compelling the use of reserves to cover shortfalls and may lead to drastic cuts in programs and personnel. The net income ratio is calculated by dividing the change in unrestricted assets from the beginning to the end of the year (net operating revenue after expenses) by total unrestricted revenues. In 2005, UNC-CH had net operating revenue of $159 million, total revenues of $1.8 billion, and a net income ratio of 8.5 percent. The target for the net income ratio is at least 2 percent to 4 percent over three or more years. This ratio constitutes only 10 percent of the CFI, but it directly affects the results of the other three ratios that account for the other 90 percent.

3. *Return on Net Assets Ratio.* The return on net assets indicates whether the institution's total assets, restricted and unrestricted, are growing or shrinking. The ratio divides the change in total net assets from the beginning of the year to the end by the total net assets at the beginning of the year. The return on net assets ratio is more comprehensive than the net income ratio just discussed because the former includes everything that happened over the year: not only net income from operations but also investments in plant, endowment appreciation, receipt of major gifts, and other events. UNC-CH had a return on net assets ratio of 16.3 percent in 2005 based on a change in net assets of $366 million and total net assets of $2.2 billion. An acceptable ratio for return on net assets starts at about 3 percent to 4 percent above inflation. With annual inflation averaging 3 percent in recent years, the target becomes 6 percent to 7 percent. This ratio constitutes 20 percent of the CFI.

---

[8] Expendable net assets are calculated by deducting property, plant and equipment from the total of unrestricted and temporarily restricted assets at the end of the year and long-term debt.

[9] University of North Carolina at Chapel Hill, Audit and Finance Committee, *Comprehensive Annual Financial Report* (January 25, 2006).

4. *Viability Ratio*. The viability ratio measures the extent to which the institution could pay off its total debt with expendable assets. It is a key ratio for the financial markets and banks when they consider the creditworthiness of institutions proposing to issue new bonds. The ratio is determined by taking the expendable net assets that an institution could spend on operations and dividing them by long-term debt. UNC-CH had expendable net assets of $1.2 billion and long-term debt of $489 million in 2005 that yielded a viability ratio of 2.5. The target is 1.25 or above. As the viability ratio falls below that, an institution's capacity to respond to financial emergencies and opportunities diminishes, as does the willingness of external sources to provide new capital. This ratio constitutes 35 percent of the CFI.

Each computed ratio is divided by a fixed "strength factor" to create a score between -1 and +10. The four scores are weighted and summed to create a total score for the CFI, also between -1 and +10. Exhibit 4.1 illustrates how UNC-CH calculated its CFI using the ratios and weights described earlier.

Exhibit 4.1: Sample CFI Score

University of North Carolina at Chapel Hill (2005)						
Ratio	Target	Result	/Strength Factor	= Raw Score (10 = maximum)	X Weight	= Weighted Score
Primary reserve	>.40	.71	.133	5.34	35%	1.87
Net income	2-4%	8.5%	.07	10.00	10%	1.00
Return on net assets	6-7%	16.4%	.02	8.18	20%	1.84
Viability	>1.25	2.47	.417	5.92	35%	2.07
					CFI	6.58

A CFI score or 9 to 10 indicates that the institution has the abundant resources to achieve even a robust mission. A score of 7 to 8 suggests that the institution has the financial flexibility to be able to experiment with new initiatives. Scores of 5 to 6 mean that the institution has some capacity to focus resources in order to compete successfully in the future. Institutions with scores around 3 to 4 need to direct resources to transform their programs and operations so that financial health can be improved. A CFI score of 3 is the minimum needed for financial health and stability. Less than 3 indicates a need for significant reengineering and retrenchment, and even assessing the viability of the institution for survival if the score drops below 0.

UNC-CH's CFI of 6.5 in 2005 clearly exceeds the threshold of 3 — although it had been as low as 3.8 as recently as 2004. The institution is poised to use resources to gain competitive advantage in the future. A comparison that UNC-CH made with peer institutions offered an additional perspective. In 2005, the CFI at the University of Michigan was about 9.4, North Carolina State University 3.3, and the University of Virginia 9.0.

Working with the Austen Group, the Council of Independent Colleges (CIC) developed the Financial Indicators Tool (FIT) that contains information on five indicators of financial vitality for small and mid-sized private colleges and universities. Four of the indicators are commonly used financial ratios that comprise the CFI. The FIT uses data from two publicly available sources: (1) the Integrated Postsecondary Education Data System (IPEDS), the major national source of public information on postsecondary institutions provided by the National Center for Education Statistics; and (2) institutional financial statements as reported on IRS Form 990 and made available by GuideStar.[10]

Effective Indicators. What makes an effective set of strategic indicators for a college or university? The first test is whether the set focuses on issues that matter to the institution. For all institutions, this would include the prime sources and uses of funds and net operating results. For example, a faculty concerned with protecting the academic program against inroads by administrative overhead might look at the proportions of the budget committed to instruction (mainly faculty salaries) and academic support (the library). Public universities also might be concerned about state appropriations and levels of support from the affiliated foundation. An independent college might want to study liquidity and changes in net tuition after deducting institutional financial aid.

Second, the indicators should flow from the mission and strategic plan and be used to evaluate progress toward their accomplishment. For example, a community college with a new student-retention initiative in its strategic plan would track corresponding sets of strategic indicators to measure success or failure of that component of the plan.

A third test is to determine whether a reasonable cause-and-effect relationship exists between institutional action and movement in the indicators. Some indicators may be clearly attributed to what the institution does — if it sets an enrollment ceiling or hires a large proportion of part-time faculty. Others may be partly linked or not linked at all, and might include the proportion of accepted students who enroll.

Fourth, the indicators should be used to measure trends over time and contain targets. It matters little if student satisfaction with dining services has increased 10 percent this academic year. More important are the degree to which student satisfaction has increased or decreased in five years and the target the institution is trying to reach.

Fifth, to capture the attention of presidents, trustees, and legislators, the institution should adopt no more than 15 to 20 indicators at the executive or top level of analysis. Subsidiary indicators that detail each of the main ones may be added, of course. For example, institutional grant aid as a percentage of student tuition and fees might be a main indicator (the classic "tuition discount.") Subsidiary indicators might include net tuition after discounting, the percentage of students on grant aid and total aid including work and loan components, and the percentage of aided students by class.

---

[10] The Austen Group, *Financial Indicators Tool (FIT)*, (Washington, D.C.: Council of Independent Colleges, 2005).

Finally, the institution should regularly report progress on the indicators with analyses of data and projections for the future. If tuition discounting increases, what does that mean for the strategic plan and budget, and what is the discount likely to be in future?

Step 7: Evaluation

The acronym CASH suggests the four ways an institution can evaluate its strategic indicators: *Comparatively* with similar institutions, with reference to a national *average* (or median) or industry *standard*, and *historically* within the same institution over time.

Comparison. A comparison group provides a context for institutional data. An institution satisfied with progress made on faculty salaries, for example, may be disappointed after finding out what other colleges and universities are paying. There are at least three bases for comparison:

- *Peer institutions* are similar in terms of such factors as institutional mission, public or independent, degree programs, enrollment, expenditures per student, and selectivity.[11] Public colleges and universities frequently compare themselves with other institutions in their athletic conferences or the state system.

- *Aspirant institutions* represent goals. These institutions have similar missions and educational programs, but they also have larger budgets and endowments, are more selective, and have better academic reputations and other desirable characteristics. The aim of the institution doing the comparison is to use the improvements promised in the strategic plan to transform itself into a peer of the current aspirants.

- *Competitor institutions* are rivals, most often for students but also for faculty, research grants, and capital gifts. Competitors may vary considerably in some of the same qualities that were used to select peers and aspirants. A common example is that of public universities, which might be prime competitors in terms of students and faculty but are not otherwise similar enough to be peers or even aspirants.

Finding the right comparison group is tricky. The group should be large enough (ten or more) to provide significant data and overcome differences in accounting procedures, such as recognition of depreciation or expenditures recognized as instruction versus institutional support) that often invalidate single-institution comparisons.[12] Nevertheless, it is often tempting to select "the" institution to which comparisons are made, especially if there is a long history of competition and rivalry. Guilford College, for example, has formal peer and aspirant groups, but much of the campus naturally looks to Earlham College in Indiana, because of its common Quaker roots and academic excellence, and to Elon University for a common benchmark in North Carolina and a prime admissions competitor. Furthermore, finding peers and aspirants that are similar on all or most of the factors often is difficult. For example, the growth of adult degree programs at many institutions but not at others complicates the selection.

---

[11] Thomas Anderes, "Using Peer Institutions in Financial and Budgetary Analysis," in Lucie Lapovsky and Mary P. McKeown-Moak, (eds.) *Roles and Responsibilities of the Chief Financial Officer* (San Francisco; Jossey-Bass, 1999), pp. 117-123.

[12] See a report published by Harvard's Kennedy School of Government, *What Does Operating Income Really Mean? An Analysis of the Financial Statements of Private Colleges and Universities* (May 2004).

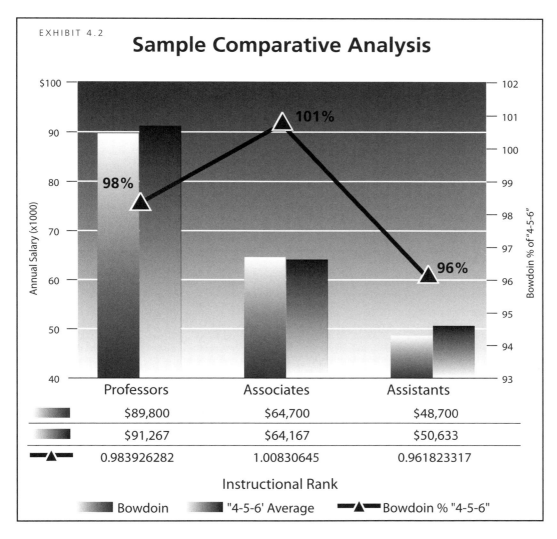

EXHIBIT 4.2

Sample Comparative Analysis

Instructional Rank	Professors	Associates	Assistants
Bowdoin	$89,800	$64,700	$48,700
"4-5-6" Average	$91,267	$64,167	$50,633
Bowdoin % "4-5-6"	0.983926282	1.00830645	0.961823317

Many colleges and universities identify different peer groups for different special purposes. An institution may reference a regional group for admissions and a local group (possibly including corporate and government competitors) for support-staff salaries. However, encouraging such variation for the overall budget may mean that the comparison institutions are not making the same trade-offs between significant budget items such as student fees, endowment spending, faculty salaries, and major maintenance expenses that you are. Comparing salaries against the first ten colleges on the list and major maintenance against the next ten on the same list may be misleading.

Exhibit 4.2 shows a sample comparison of faculty salaries against a group of peer colleges. In this case, Bowdoin College compared itself with an 18-college group of national liberal arts colleges with which it competed for students and faculty. The target was to meet the average of the fourth, fifth, and sixth highest salaries (hence the "4-5-6" target) or 75th percentile among the 18 colleges at each rank. It shows that the college exceeded the targets for associate professors (101 percent) but fell behind for professors (98 percent) and assistant professors (96 percent).

The Integrated Postsecondary Education Data System (IPEDS) is a system of federally sponsored surveys designed to collect data from all U.S. colleges and universities. IPEDS collects institution-level data in such areas as enrollment, program completion, faculty, staff, and finances.[13] The IPEDS Peer Analysis System is a Web-based tool that can be used to compare a postsecondary institution of the user's choice to a group of self-selected peers. It allows searches for institutional peers by location, program, or degree offerings — either alone or in combination.

While a comparison group is most useful for general perspective, institutions also may index selected parts of the budget to the peer group. For example, during the past decade, Williams College charged its student fees based on the median of its competitor group. Allegheny, Sarah Lawrence, and other colleges set faculty salaries to maintain a certain position within their comparison groups. Bowdoin College strove to keep faculty salaries at the 75th percentile within its 18-college comparison group. Less-affluent Guilford College targets the 50th percentile of its group.

Averages. National averages by different size of institution and control can be gathered through the annual IPEDS survey data. Data can be obtained for public and independent research universities, comprehensive institutions, undergraduate colleges, and community colleges. Benchmarking information derived from IPEDS data also is readily available from other sources, such as AGB, the Council of Independent Colleges (CIC), and the National Association of College and University Business Officers. Another data exchange is offered by the Associated New American Colleges, a group of 19 small to mid-sized comprehensive colleges and universities dedicated to the integration of liberal arts and professional studies.[14] Finally, Higher Education Data Sharing is a consortium of 141 institutions that share data designed to advance planning, management, and institutional research.[15] Exhibit 4.3 is a sample report from AGB's Benchmarking Service that shows how averages provide a valuable comparative perspective on student diversity.

Standards. Standards can be derived from the institution's own goals in the strategic plan, from ratings needed to achieve a certain bond rating or bond covenant, or from applied industry standards. Examples:

· The strategic plan calls for the six-year graduation rate to reach 75 percent within three years.

· A bond covenant may require the institution to maintain a 0.75 ratio between expendable funds available for debt service (cash, cash equivalents, and board-designated endowment) and total debt.

· APPA: The Association of Higher Education Facilities Officers promulgates a standard for deferred maintenance with its Facility Condition Index (FCI):

$$\mathbf{FCI} = \frac{\$ \text{ amount of deferred maintenance}}{\$ \text{ amount replacement value of plant (buildings)}}$$

[13] Information about the IPEDS surveys and tools can be found at *www.nces.ed.gov/ipeds*

[14] See *www.anac.vir.org*

[15] See *www.e-heds.org*

Exhibit 4.3: Student Diversity Comparisons

	Focus Institution			Comparison Group		
	Full-time %	Part-time %	All %	Full-time %	Part-time %	All %
Men						
Nonresident Alien	3.8	33.3	3.9	3.5	4.6	3.3
Black Non-Hispanic	5.1	0.0	5.0	9.2	10.7	10.1
American Indian/Alaskan Native	0.8	0.0	0.8	0.5	0.7	0.5
Asian or Pacific Islander	8.7	0.0	8.7	2.8	2.6	2.7
Hispanic	5.3	0.0	5.3	3.6	3.2	3.5
White Non-Hispanic	74.6	66.7	74.6	74.2	65.5	72.3
Ethnicity unknown	1.8	0.0	1.8	6.1	12.8	7.7
Total	**100**	**100**	**100**	**100**	**100**	**100**
Total N (headcount)	851	3	854	113,825	15,695	129,520
Women						
Nonresident Alien	2.4	50.0	2.8	3.1	4.5	3.0
Black Non-Hispanic	5.8	0.0	5.7	9.9	10.3	10.0
American Indian/Alaskan Native	0.7	0.0	0.7	0.4	0.3	0.4
Asian or Pacific Islander	13.6	0.0	13.5	3.8	1.9	3.8
Hispanic	6.1	16.7	6.2	4.0	3.5	3.9
White Non-Hispanic	68.8	33.3	68.5	72.6	66.0	72.2
Ethnicity unknown	2.6	0.0	2.6	6.2	13.5	6.6
Total	**100**	**100**	**100**	**100**	**100**	**100**
Total N (headcount)	817	6	823	159,027	25,347	184,374
Combined						
Nonresident Alien	3.1	44.4	3.3	3.4	4.8	3.3
Black Non-Hispanic	5.4	0.0	5.4	10.3	10.7	10.4
American Indian/Alaskan Native	0.8	0.0	0.8	0.5	0.4	0.5
Asian or Pacific Islander	11.1	0.0	11.0	3.6	2.3	3.5
Hispanic	5.7	11.1	5.7	3.9	3.5	3.9
White Non-Hispanic	71.8	44.4	71.6	72.3	65.2	71.9
Ethnicity unknown	2.2	0.0	2.1	6.1	13.1	6.6
Total	**100**	**100**	**100**	**100**	**100**	**100**
Total N (headcount)	1,668	9	1,677	272,852	41,042	313,894

Thus, a campus with $5 million of deferred maintenance and a replacement value of $100 million would have an FCI of .05. According to APPA, an FCI below .05 is "good," between .05 and .10 is "fair," and over .10 is "poor."[16]

---

[16] California Community Colleges, Association of Chief Business Officials Task Force, *Facilities Update* (October 22, 2001). See also: Robert Brooks, "History of the Facilities Condition Index," *Facilities Manager* (July/August 2004), pp. 31-33.

Historical Analysis. This analysis allows the college or university to detect its own shifting revenue dependencies and expense priorities over time. Exhibit 4.4 illustrates a historical analysis of total endowment and endowment per student. It reveals that total endowment has increased about 800 percent over 20 years, while endowment per student, a better indicator of institutional wealth, rose more slowly at 730 percent.

At least three to five years of consistently defined and reported data are needed for a good historical analysis. Shifting definitions of functional categories can undermine a historical analysis. Such categories that are prone to shift include instruction and institutional support; accounting standards that changed the format of financial statements and recognition of pledges, especially Financial Accounting Standards (FAS) 116 and 117 for independent institutions (1995 forward) and Governmental Accounting Standards (GAS) 34 and 35 for public institutions (2001 forward); and rules for writing off accounts and pledges receivable or for depreciation of buildings.

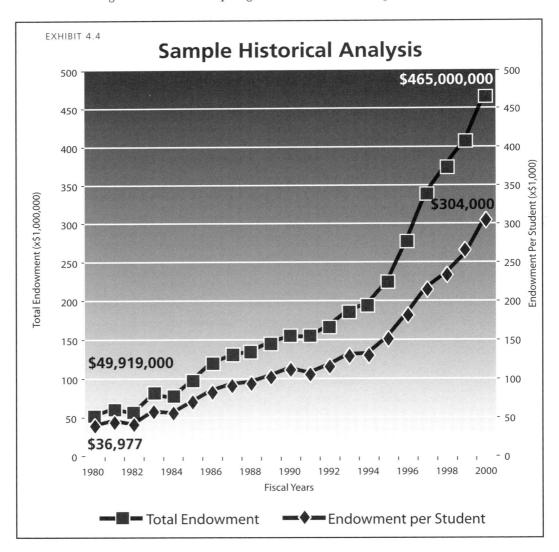

EXHIBIT 4.4

Exhibit 4.5: Sample Indicators and Evalution

Continuing Goal 2: Expand our academic community			
Internal Indicator	**Omega College FY10 Goal**	**Omega College 2005**	**Omega College 2004**
1. Percentage of students involved in inter-institutional programs *	8%	1%	1%
2. Percentage of total student credit hours taught to non-Omega College inter-institutional students	5%	11 (Fall 2005) = 1%	1%
3. Percentage of non-degree student credit hours	5%	1%	1%
4. Admission yield for traditional students	30%	26%	26%
5. Percentage of first-year traditional cohort that is retained to junior year	70%	64%	65%

Comparative Indicator	Omega College FY 10 Goal	Omega College 2005	Omega College 2004	Peer Average		Aspirant Average	
				Range	Rank (of 14)	Range	Rank (of 9)
6. Traditional student enrollment	1,500	1,297	1,244	2,119		2,239	
				923-3,308	8	1,260-2,891	7
7. Nontraditional student enrollment	1,700	1,299	1,181	651		85	
				113-1,860	4	5-207	2
8. First-year retention rate (traditional students)	80%	73%	76%	80%		86%	
				67%-93%	9	76%-92%	7
9. Average SAT	1,225	1,137	1,145	1,116		1,214	
				1,030-1,210	8	1,050-1,330	7
10. Percentage of traditional students in top 10% of high school class	25%	13%	15%	30%		34%	
				16%-44%	9	7%-68%	9

* More students are enrolled in spring than in fall.

Exhibit 4.5 shows how institutions can evaluate strategic indicators. The chart lists the continuing goal, the related strategic indicators, where the institution is now and where it hopes to be over a specified time period, and how the institution compares with its aspirant and peer groups. A range within these groups often is useful information because reporting only the median or average can be deceptive when a few institutions in the comparison group are significantly higher or lower.

Analysis. The major focus of this goal is to grow enrollment to 3,200 by 2010. For both the traditional and nontraditional populations, the college seems to be on target to reach the respective head-count goals of 1,500 and 1,700 by FY 2010. The traditional totals are lower than the averages of peer and aspirant groups, while the nontraditional totals are higher.

Part of enrollment growth projections is new admissions — where the yield rate (percentage of admitted students who enroll) of 26 percent is below the goal of 30 percent. Average SAT scores (1,137-1,145) currently are not quite as close to the 2010 goal of 1,225, but the goal is higher than the averages of peers (1,116) and aspirants (1,214). The chart reveals that the college is not performing very well in its efforts to increase the enrollment of traditional students in the top 10 percent of their high school class. The 2004-05 rates of 13 percent to 15 percent are below the 2010 goal of 25 percent and the averages of peers (40 percent) and aspirants (35 percent).

Another aspect of the analysis is the retention of current students: The percentages of traditional students retained to sophomore year — 73 percent to 76 percent — and to the junior year — 64 percent to 65 percent — already approach the 2010 goals of 80 percent and 70 percent.) Inter-institutional cooperation on paper looks like a priority, but less than 1 percent of traditional students enroll for classes at other institutions compared with an 8 percent goal.

Step 8: Action Steps

Many planning processes stumble at this point. Core values, mission, goals, and objectives are all dramatic parts of the plan and are often exciting and even inspirational. They often form the basis of major presidential addresses, capital campaign statements, and presentations to trustees, legislators, and other friends of the institution.

Means, however, are far less interesting. The means to those ends require appropriate programs, services, and staff to implement them. Means are more about management of resources than the kind of leadership that presidents and trustees offer, as they involve detailed project-management decisions that range from personnel to schedules to financing. Means, or their implementation, also can derail the strategic plan if its ends are more ambitious than the institution can afford or is able to achieve. Ambitious plans receive publicity and credit; detailed implementation schedules do not and, in fact, will attract blame if they cause the plan to be reconsidered or derailed. For these reasons, many colleges and universities adopt plans without thinking through how to accomplish them.

Importance. "You can't get there from here" is the punch line of a hoary joke about getting directions in rural America, but the conundrum emerges as an essential issue in terms of judging a plan's feasibility. Goals, objectives, and other ends that seem eminently doable at first often become impossible when weighing the action steps, timelines, and responsible persons and offices needed to achieve the ends. What goes wrong? Usually, the action steps are more complex and numerous than expected, or the project timelines are too ambitious or beyond the capacities of those assigned to execute them. Operational commitments may supersede the new demands the plan brings.

Characteristics. Objectives can entail anywhere from 5 to 20 action steps, each of which may have subsidiary tasks. Action steps are explicit statements: "Contact five potential colleges or universities to participate in the instructional technology consortium." They are means to the ends and not the ends themselves. A test for detecting whether an action step is a means or an end is to ask about the action step, "Why are we doing this?" The answer should be the objective that is connected to the action step.

Exhibit 4.6 Sample Action Steps

Continuing Goal 2: Expand our academic community						
Strategic Priority 2-1: Develop and strengthen alliances with other institutions.						
OBJECTIVE: By 2010, Omega College will have alliances with at least three colleges and universities to create specialized undergraduate opportunities and/or cooperative graduate degrees.						
	Starting Semester	**Ending Semester**	**Primary Responsibility**	**Secondary Responsibility**	**Trustee Committee**	**Faculty Committee**
1. Identify majors that are viable candidates for institutional alliances.	2005 Fall	2006 Spring	Academic Dean	Department Chairs	Academic Affairs	Educational Policy
2. Report priority for institutional alliances to president and Strategic Long-Range Planning Committee.	2006 Spring	2006 Fall	Academic Dean	Department Chairs	Academic Affairs	Educational Policy
3. Develop articulation agreements for general education requirements with accredited colleges and universities within 50 miles.	2007 Fall	2008 Spring	Academic Dean	Department Chairs	Academic Affairs	Educational Policy
4. Identify and evaluate partners to develop on-site, supervised graduate courses utilizing faculty and materials delivered via the Internet.	2008 Fall	2009 Spring	President	Academic Dean	Academic Affairs	Educational Policy
5. Report priority list for institutional alliances to SLRP.	2009 Spring	2010 Spring	President	Department Chairs	Academic Affairs	Educational Policy
6. Implement alliances.	2007 Fall	2010 Spring	Academic Dean	Department Chairs	Academic Affairs	Educational Policy

Action steps are assigned to specific individuals and offices. For an institutionwide plan, each action step should be the responsibility of a single senior officer who then will organize his or her division for implementation. It also is helpful to enlist oversight committees composed of trustees, faculty, and other constituencies. Finally, action steps are time-specific, with starting and completion dates typically expressed in months or semesters.

Examples. Exhibit 4.6 displays sample action steps with timelines and areas of responsibility.

Campus Master Plan. A crucial action step in many strategic plans is the campus master plan. The campus master plan focuses on buildings and space and lays out the strategic plan's impact on facilities and land. Assessment of buildings involves an examination of architectural character, condition, and usability; how adaptable they are to programmatic needs; the suitability of the site; and code compliance. Assessment of space includes uses of existing space, deficiencies and surpluses for each academic and administrative program, and future space requirements for various enrollment scenarios. The campus master plan aims to achieve recognizable entrances, identifiable centers, defined edges, organized circulation, efficient maintenance, and simplicity of design.[17]

A campus master plan begins with principles that guide the effort. Carnegie Mellon University set 13 principles for its plan, including the following:

- The campus-like nature of the university's open space is a strong component of its physical environment, and therefore the university shall be its steward. Campus green space shall be protected, and the quality shall be enhanced.

- Transportation routes through and around the campus shall facilitate the movement of pedestrians, vehicles, and materials to their destinations. Where pedestrians and vehicles conflict, pedestrian needs take priority.

- Sites for future buildings and open spaces shall be identified and preserved for the most appropriate use.

- Campus buildings and open spaces shall be designed with regard to their environmental impact.

- The campus environment shall be enhanced by quality public art.[18]

These principles must be part of a specific scope of work between the institution and the master planners, especially if the plan is outsourced.[19] The scope also should include the budget, key personnel contracted to work on the project, and timelines for planning, community involvement, and trustee review. If the institution has special areas of focus, such as sustainability, landscaping, or residential life, the master plan should specifically address these. Additionally, the information technology implications of the plan should be acknowledged.

Expectations about level of detail should be clarified early in the master plan. At one extreme, a master plan may lay out broad principles and areas of the campus for development. At the other extreme, the master plan may site specific academic and residential buildings, programs, and departments within buildings.

The wide range of issues addressed by a master plan is exemplified in the table of contents of the plan developed for Rhode Island College, as shown in Exhibit 4.7.

Step 9: Revenues and Costs

Undoubtedly, the most significant determinant of the strategic plan's feasibility is its affordability. Does the institution have the current revenues to cover the costs of the plan? Does the plan itself generate new revenue from expansion, a capital campaign, or state appropriations? A plan need not aim to be profitable, but the combination of existing and new revenue must equal or exceed the costs the plan envisions.

---

[17] Van Yahres Associates, "Campus Master Plan for Guilford College" (April 2005).

[18] *Carnegie Mellon Campus Plan* (2002), Attachment A2, pp. 45–47.

[19] Master planners are often independent firms or consultants who have worked with a wide range of institutions on full master plans or on particular aspects such as environmental impacts or landscape management. Large institutions have campus-planning units within their facilities departments that can do master plans on their own or work with consultants. Whether master planning is internal or outsourced, the institution's leadership must be actively involved throughout the process.

Exhibit: 4.7: Master Plan Table of Contents

College Master Plans[20]		
1. Executive Summary	**3. Unifying the Campus**	**5. Traffic and Parking**
Introduction	Introduction and Goals	Goals
Recommendations	Location and Setting	Existing Conditions
Implementation	Campus Character and Organization	Existing Circulation
2. Introduction	Arrival Sequence	Existing Parking
Planning Process	Roadways and Parking Lots	Recommendations
History	Pathways	**6. Signage and Identity**
The Plan	Recommendations	Existing Conditions
Guiding Principles	**4. East Campus Occupancy**	Recommendations
	Goals	**7. Implementation**
	Existing Campus Space	Focus Areas
	Space Needs and Issues	Budgets
	Alternatives for East Campus	Appendix
	Impact on Campus Core	

Revenues. Revenue sources and estimates for the plan will depend on the strategic priorities and actions proposed to achieve them. If a college proposes to increase enrollment in order to become more efficient or enhance diversity, for example, net revenues will depend largely on estimates of enrollment and student tuition and fees. Exhibit 4.8 shows the questions that might drive such an analysis.

Exhibit 4.8: Analysis of Enrollment and Student Fees

Enrollment	Student Tuition And Fees
• What are the estimated numbers of new students by year and type of student (undergraduate, graduate, adult)?	• What are assumed gross fees per student by year and type of student?
• What are the estimates for transfer students by year and type?	• Do we charge a comprehensive fee or a per-credit charge?
• Impact on student profiles in terms of gender, race, need, and other characteristics?	• What is the percentage of the students on financial aid by year and type of student?
• Assumptions about the percentage of students living on and off campus?	• What is the dollar value of the average aid package by year and type of student?
• What are the retention rates by year and type?	• Proportions of the aid package in institutional grants, loans, and work-study?
• What are the estimates on full-time equivalent and headcount bases?	• What are the other costs associated with growth (new faculty, admissions and marketing, student housing, classrooms and offices?) Per student? Per credit hour?
• What are the graduation rates by year and type of student?	• What is the net revenue per student by year and type of student?

[20] Rhode Island College, "College Master Plan," *www.ric.edu/masterplan/table_contents.html* (accessed February 2006.)

Other new revenues can come from increased annual giving and state aid, the proceeds from a capital campaign, and debt (especially if there is a new revenue stream associated with the plan.) The fair attribution of new revenues to the plan versus other factors is a complex but essential undertaking.

Costs. Costs can be divided into personnel and non-personnel costs. Personnel costs may be difficult to gauge for the following reasons:

- The institution must decide what costs are attributable to the plan. For example, how does the registrar in an "enrollment growth" strategy divide his or her time and salary between new and current students?

- The institution must decide how to allocate personnel costs by type of student. A traditional student paying a comprehensive fee uses more services and incurs more costs than a part-time adult student. Such an allocation most likely will require a survey of academic support (library, informational technology, academic skills) and student services (registrar, counseling and health services, and the like) to determine use by type of student.

- What percentage of personnel costs are new costs for consultants and additional staff, and which are "in kind" costs, given that faculty and staff are expected to engage in planning as part of their jobs?

Non-personnel costs also must be identified and allocated. In some cases, this task will be fairly straightforward. The academic dean or business office can estimate the administrative and other expenses associated with hiring new faculty. In other cases, the costs are sizable, institutionwide, and more difficult to allocate. An example is an administrative software conversion mandated by the plan where the non-personnel costs of the software purchase, installation, and training are dwarfed by the personnel costs of staff involved in the conversion. However, as with personnel costs, non-personnel costs incurred by departments in support of the plan probably will need a detailed survey to be known and allocated to the plan.

Estimating Revenues and Costs. Compiling these estimates is an iterative process, in which costs and revenues are computed and then adjusted up or down until revenues equal or exceed costs. For example, the first iteration might result in $10 million in costs and only $8 million in revenue. Subsequent iterations might deal with the gap by increasing enrollment and student fees, hiking the endowment spending rate, lowering the benchmarks for faculty and staff salary increases, and/or deferring new programs, capital projects, and their related debt service. Each of these components may be adjusted until the plan's financing is brought into balance.

Costs and revenues typically are computed beginning with the lowest level in the plan — for individual action steps or tasks within action steps. That way, the related resources can be estimated clearly and concretely.

Task 1: Costs by Action Step. If the objective is to expand enrollment, the action step taken to identify majors suitable for an inter-institutional alliance and the $12,000 total cost related to that task might include the personnel costs of a consultant's time ($5,000) and the non-personnel costs of expenses ($5,000) and travel/miscellaneous ($2,000.)

Exhibit 4.9: Costs By Objective

Continuing Goal 2: Expand our Academic Community					$930,000
Strategic Priority 2-1: Develop and strengthen alliances with other institutions.					**$610,000**
OBJECTIVE					
1. By 2010, Omega College will have alliances with at least three colleges and universities to create specialized undergraduate opportunities and/or cooperative graduate degrees.					**$295,000**
	FY 2006-07	FY 2007-08	FY 2008-09	FY 2009-10	TOTALS
Action Steps					
1. Identify majors that are viable candidates for institutional alliances.	$10,000	$2,000			$12,000
2. Report priority list for institutional alliances to president and Strategic Long-Range Planning Committee.	$1,000				$1,000
3. Develop articulation agreements for general education requirements with accredited colleges and universities within 50 miles.		$15,000			$15,000
4. Identify and evaluate partners to develop on-site supervised graduate courses utilizing faculty and materials delivered via the Internet.			$10,000		$10,000
5. Report priority list for institutional alliances to SLRP.				$2,500	$2,500
6. Implement alliances.	$50,000	$60,000	$70,000	$75,000	$255,000

Task 2: Costs by Objective. Resulting financial estimates by action step are rolled up to the objective related to the action steps. Thus, if the five action steps of Objective X carry a total cost of $35,000, that becomes the total cost of Objective X. The roll-up continues by compiling the costs of all the objectives to estimate the costs of the goal — and upward to higher levels in the plan in order to compute totals by year and for the entire plan. This roll-up process is illustrated in Exhibit 4.9, where a cost of $295,000 for Objective 1 is added to the costs of other parts of the plan (not shown on the exhibit). The total is $610,000 for the strategic priority and $930,000 for the continuing goal.

Task 3: Total Revenues and Costs. Finally, the five goals in the plan might sum to $14.7 million in costs and, by the same stepwise method, $16.2 million in revenue as shown in Exhibit 4.10 (page 64). This plan also results in a $1.5 million operating gain, but this is not likely to be realized. An almost inexorable law of planning is that projected revenues are almost always lower than expected and expenses higher than expected.

Step 10: Assessment

A strategic plan is a dynamic statement of purpose and direction that must be periodically assessed and changed, if necessary. The assessment should use a variety of data sources and should be a continuous process monitored by the board and chief executive.

Issues. Among the issues an assessment might address are the following:

- Were objectives met on time and within budget?

Exhibit 4.10: Total Plan Revenues and Costs

Operating Revenue by Source			
Fiscal Year	Increased Endowment Returns	Enrollment Growth Net Revenue	Total New Revenue
2004-05	0	0	0
2005-06	0	1,500	1,500
2006-07	46	2,374	2,420
2007-08	218	3,106	3,324
2008-09	343	3,726	4,069
2009-10	550	4,360	4,910
Total	1,157	15,066	16,223

Operating Expenses by Function and Net						
Fiscal Year	New Debt Service on $5 million	Faculty Salary Increases to Market	Other Costs	Total New Costs From Plan	Net Operating Gain/(Loss)	Cumulative Gain (Loss)
2004-05	0	0	216	216	(216)	(216)
2005-06	0	282	874	1,156	344	128
2006-07	0	646	1,361	2,007	413	541
2007-08	0	1,101	1,598	2,699	625	1,166
2008-09	338	1,646	1,862	3,846	223	1,389
2009-10	338	2,299	2,121	4,758	152	1,541
Total	676	5,974	8,031	14,682	1,541	

- Have action steps been completed on time and within budget?

- Do staffing levels and assignments for the action steps continue to make sense in terms of workload and effectiveness?

- Are there unexpected challenges and opportunities that affect the plan, especially new strategies by competitors?

- Has timely progress been made on targets expressed in the strategic indicators and linked to the objectives and goals?

- Have financial assumptions underlying the plan come true?

Strategic Gap. A core reason why plans fail is the strategic gap between lofty ends and the tedious but essential means. This can occur during the planning process when action steps and financing either are not capably executed or are ignored. It's a bad sign if the plan is adopted — often to maintain morale and momentum — even though its total cost may far exceed foreseeable resources. A strategic gap also can occur during implementation. For example, how should the institution deal with the strategic gap if the plan assumes $20 million in capital giving to support construction of a new student center but raises only $10 million?

The best way is obvious: to close the gap during plan development by lowering expectations or finding new resources. This possibility should be an explicit part of the planning process from the beginning so that the community is not blindsided or disappointed later. Other techniques:

· Ends should be prioritized in advance so that shortfalls in financing result in more-predictable adjustments to less-important goals and objectives.

· Visible and practical "what if" scenarios should be considered during and after planning to anticipate possible strategic gaps.

· The plan's duration may be extended to allow more time to accomplish the plan's ends or to obtain adequate resources.

· Goals and objectives can be preserved, but more economical action steps may be selected to accomplish them.

Role of the Chief Executive. The chief executive leads the assessment process by approving the methods, providing the resources, and being receptive to negative feedback. "Seduction of the leader" occurs when subordinates are reluctant to share the truth with the boss because of fear of reprisal, desire not to hurt or offend, or to curry favor. By encouraging truth-telling and constructive criticism, the chief executive signals to the college or university community that accurate assessment and change for the better are planning priorities.

The chief executive also should ensure that the annual performance appraisal of those responsible for implementing the plan is based, in part, on their degree of success. Thus, if a dean has primary responsibility for an educational goal with specific strategic indicators, those indicators are part of that dean's performance appraisal. The chief executive's own appraisal should reflect the results of assessment of the overall plan.

Role of the Governing Board. The governing board has a prominent role in assessing execution of the strategic plan. Doing so is fundamental to its exercise of governance and fiduciary responsibility. Board commitment to assess the plan is a significant determinant of its success. According to Kay Sprinkel Grace, author and consultant on philanthropy, board members may fulfill that responsibility by doing the following:

· ensuring that all board committees fulfill the goals and objectives in their area of jurisdiction (for example, the development committee meets its fund-raising responsibilities);

· using the plan as the basis for recruitment of community members whose expertise and experience will help the institution achieve its goals;

· requiring committee chairs and senior management to refer to the plan in all reporting at board meetings;

· asking for a written update on the plan quarterly or semiannually from the staff;

Exhibit 4.11 Questions Trustees Should Ask About the Strategic Plan

Objectives and Goals of the Plan
1. Does the plan provide a clear vision of what the institution will look like if the plan is accomplished?
2. To what extent are the objectives and action steps linked directly to the goals outlined in the plan?
3. To what extent are the objectives specific in deadlines and indicators (with comparative benchmarks) so that their accomplishment is evident?
4. Is the plan supported by a feasible long range financial plan (including revenue, fund-raising targets, and full costs?) Is there a supporting campus master plan?
5. To what extent can the plan and long range financial plan be linked to annual budgets?

Action Steps of the Plan
6. Are the action steps specific, discrete tasks that provide concrete guidance to those responsible for carrying them out?
7. Do the action steps convey clear assignments of leadership responsibility to one specific person or office?
8. Have the action steps been reviewed by internal and external stakeholders (especially faculty for the curriculum) for impacts on workload and feasibility?

The Overall Plan
9. Is the overall plan based on and report specific data both on the status quo situation and on proposed future directions?
10. Does the overall plan reflect a practical statement of what the institution might reasonably accomplish in the next five to seven years?
11. Does the overall plan have direct links to the core values of the institution?
12. Is the plan exciting to read? Will it inspire active support?
13. Does the overall plan represent the opinions and the best interests of the educational community?
14. Does the overall plan make clear the hard choices among competing priorities? Does it propose elimination of existing programs or services?
15. Are the competitive advantages of the plan clearly laid out?
16. Does the plan specify regular assessment and revisions based on new data and circumstances?

- establishing a planning committee or task force responsible for ongoing monitoring of the plan; and

- implementing regular plan updates that reflect new opportunities or constraints or sudden changes in staffing, funding sources, or other resources.[21]

Additionally, the governing board might organize meetings around one or two key goals. That way, they are kept informed about progress and encouraged to discuss alternatives. These meetings should occur not only during implementation but also while the plan is being developed.

Exhibit 4.11 suggests some questions trustees should ask about the strategic plan.

---

[21] Kay Sprinkel Grace, *The Nonprofit Board's Role in Strategic Planning* (Washington, D.C.: National Center for Nonprofit Boards, 1996), pp. 19-20.

Sample Assessment

Assessment should form an official part of the plan rather than an assumption. The process and timing of assessment should be explicitly stated in the plan when it is approved. A sample assessment follows:

The Strategic Long-Range Planning Committee (SLRP) is charged with "reviewing long-range plans and goals annually and with providing the institutional memory required to remain centered on the college's goals." The president should lead SLRP each spring in an assessment of the strategic plan and operational priorities to evaluate:

· timely completion of action steps;

· progress of strategic and performance indicators toward goals, especially as they affect the academic program;

· achievement of financial targets that support the plan;

· congruence of the annual budget with plan priorities; and

· the need for changes in the content of the plan or its implementation.

The results of the assessment will be disseminated to the community for input. The president and board of trustees must approve any recommendations for material changes at the fall meeting. For the board, the strategic and performance indicators provide the best way to assess the plan without becoming mired in "how to" issues.

Exhibit 4.12 is a reformatted version of an actual quarterly assessment report from Longwood University. This excerpt focuses on student goals.[22]

Exhibit 4.12 Sample Assessment Report

1999-2000 Goals Versus Performance			
STUDENTS: Attract students who can take full advantage of, and contribute richly to, this learning-centered environment, students who are academically capable and who will benefit from the diversity of past experience and current interests among them.			
Goal Area	**Goal**	**Performance**	**Year-End Status**
Enrollment	1,020 new students	1,031	Exceeded
Quality	1,060 SAT, 3.1 GPA	1,061 SAT; 3.12 GPA	Exceeded
Diversity	15% minority enrollment	15%	Completed
Persistence	81%	78.8%	Not met
Four-Year Graduation Rate	50%	40.6%	Not met
Job Placement Rate	90th percentile	91st percentile	Exceeded

[22] Longwood University, "Strategic Planning & Goals of Longwood University," *www.longwood.edu/assessment/Mission/ Mission2002.htm* (accessed August 2006).

Buy-In and Support for the Strategic Plan

A strategic plan is only as good as its implementation. Making good on all the aims and aspirations in the plan is a complex undertaking with political and cultural implications as well as strategic and financial challenges. How does a college or university achieve buy-in and support for the plan that will facilitate its implementation?

Process Factors. Some facilitating factors involve the process by which the plan was developed and implemented. The time to start focusing on buy-in and support is when the plan is being developed, not when it's already a "done deal." The assumption underlying an effective process is that a plan developed with widespread participation is ultimately better understood and accepted. When the strategic plan touches on instruction and the academic program, faculty participation is essential. Such inclusion also improves the plan, as it reflects the realities and dreams of the

Exhibit 4.13: Process Factors

• **To gain support and credibility**	Use a widely representative planning committee to develop the plan and preserve strategic thinking. Include administrators, support staff, faculty, and students. Consider alumni and members of existing advisory boards.
• **To lower perceived risks**	Obtain and publicize strong support of the chief executive and influential members of the board and the community who become the plan's "champions."
• **To gain trustee support**	Create a counterpart trustee planning committee or planning function in an existing committee to provide board oversight, input, and support. Participate in regular assessment of the plan.
• **To focus on the facts**	Planning can be sidetracked by conventional wisdom and myths unless planners base their strategic choices on historical, projected, and comparative data about the organization and its environment. Do not waste time arguing about the facts.
• **To ensure feasibility**	Use subcommittees of stakeholders to refine "how to" parts of plan. For example, an objective to improve student engagement might involve student affairs, residential life, career planning, athletics, student government, and faculty.
• **To increase understanding and lower anxiety**	Provide the committee and the community with comparative and historical data and regular updates during plan development.
• **To inspire vision and imagination**	Allow "blue sky" thinking initially. Do not constrain grand aspirations and bold ideas too early in the process. Allow folks to demonstrate their creativity, with the understanding that financial and management realities will be imposed later.
• **To improve quality and acceptance**	Create ways for community participation in planning. Energy comes from pushing participation down to where the action is. It also avoids the planning committee being stereotyped as "true believers."
• **To make participation meaningful**	Provide education about strategic planning: key terms, definitions, examples, case studies.
• **To create sense of fun and adventure**	Celebrate key milestones in the plan's development and implementation. For example, an all-campus party to celebrate initial implementation of the plan or achievement of a significant priority.
• **To encourage participation and feedback**	Solicit input about the plan and process and be concretely responsive. Ask good questions: What were you glad to see? What were you concerned to see? What concerns do you have about conditions that might prevent success? What questions do you have about what we need to accomplish?

Exhibit 4.14: Substantive Factors

• **To create a "bias for action"**	The plan lays out the urgency for planned change. For example, the state university announces plans to open a branch campus in the same town as an independent liberal arts college.
• **To narrow the scope and show courage**	Planners often are tempted to fit everyone's wish-lists into the plan. A successful plan is clear about what the organization has chosen to do, not do, and stop doing.
• **To promote feelings of inclusion**	Be sure that the plan mentions all aspects of the organization in terms of programs (academic affairs, student services) and functions (finance, marketing) even if few become "priorities."
• **To widen comfort zone for change**	Plan reconfirms core values and "sacred ground" that are not changing. For example, that the college will remain an undergraduate, residential institution.
• **To prove feasibility**	Make the objectives SMART so that costs can be determined and assessed: Specific, Measurable, Aggressive yet achievable, Rational and relevant, Time-bound.
• **To ensure affordability**	Determine total revenue and costs of the plan, and adjust finances for the plan as needed to ensure affordability.
• **To evidence reality**	Plan connects goals and objectives to the tasks, departments, and individuals needed to implement them. Departmental budgets and performance appraisals are linked to successful implementation.
• **To preserve focus**	Do not let short-term crises or "opportunities" divert attention from the plan.
• **To demonstrate flexibility**	Plan contains a regular assessment process linked to strategic indicators for reporting, evaluation, and revision, if needed. Plan also has "what if" scenarios to deal with unexpected events and circumstances (a drastic cut in state aid, for example).
• **To create "syndrome of success"**	Plan has key objectives slated for early achievement.
• **To provide a context**	Link the strategic plan to other planning efforts. For example, the plan should be the basis of a long-range financial plan, campus master plan, annual budget, and capital campaign.
• **To prove achievement that matters**	Strategic indicators for assessment encompass not only inputs (such as student-faculty ratio or the percentage of alumni who participate in annual giving) but outputs as well (graduation rates, scores on comprehensive exams, and standardized tests).

organizational community, broadly speaking, rather than the theoretical musings of planning experts or a borrowed template from someone else's supposedly successful planning effort. Exhibit 4.13 summarizes the process factors that support successful strategic planning.

Substantive Factors. Plans come in various shapes and sizes. It is amazing how many organizations err by publishing a strategic plan without showing how much it will cost or where to find the money to pay for it. Too often, plans focus on the ends and neglect the means. In addition, they are not only technically accurate but reflect, to the extent possible, the politics and aspirations of the community. Exhibit 4.14 suggests the substantive factors behind support and buy-in for the plan.[23]

No plan can be successful without spelling out the means to achieve the mission and other ends of the plan. These action steps are specific and realistic to the extent that the institution knows their costs, schedules their completion,

---

[23] See also Jack Calereso, "How Trustees Can Own the Strategic Plan," *Trusteeship* (November/December 2005).

assigns responsibilities to individuals and departments, and involves a range of constituencies in their development and implementation. A successful plan also needs to be evaluated using strategic indicators with historical and comparative data. Whether the indicators are analyzed separately or as an index is less important than that they are identified as part of the planning process and then analyzed accurately and regularly to evaluate and improve the plan.

CHAPTER 5

Strategy and Budgets

Colleges and universities usually see their budgets as annual spending plans that identify the sources and uses of funds. Boosting revenues through higher tuition pricing or fund-raising allows institutions to expand and improve their offerings. This circular pattern led Howard Bowen to postulate "Bowen's Law" to explain the major influence on budgeting in higher education: "Universities will raise all the money they can and spend all the money they raise."[1]

Still, a budget can be strategic in that it is a fundamental statement of priorities and beliefs. It tells a story not only about how much money is earned and spent but also which goals and activities are truly most important to the institution. In short, a budget is a plan with dollar signs.

The budget also serves strategy when it is linked to the long-range financial plan underlying the institution's strategic plan. It must connect with the campus master plan and its implementation as well as with the capital campaign feasibility study in terms of potential funding by new gifts and grants. By linking money to mission, the budget helps to anticipate the revenues and costs of the strategic plan and becomes a major determinant of its overall feasibility. Financial planning requires decisions on major budget drivers, assumptions about rates of increase or decrease of resources, the forecast period (often the same as the strategic plan), and the accuracy and comparability of the data used to drive the analysis. The annual budget may thus be viewed as one year of the multiyear plan that the institution will periodically reconsider and possibly revise.[2]

This chapter delves into the concept of financial equilibrium, defining the parts of the budget and the types of strategic and management information they provide. It examines significant budget drivers, such as tuition pricing, price inflation, endowment or foundation earnings, employee salaries and fringe benefits, and maintenance, and demonstrates the connection between the annual budget and the strategic plan through long-range financial plans and planning models.

Financial Equilibrium

The concept of "financial equilibrium" means that (1) the institution has a balanced budget, (2) projected rates of change in revenues and expenses are approximately the same, (3) endowment use is limited to preserve its long-term purchasing power, and (4) the budget is not balanced by deferring maintenance or other essential expenses, thereby creating hidden liabilities.

---

[1] Howard Bowen, *The Cost of Higher Education* (San Francisco: Jossey-Bass, 1980) quoted in William F. Massy, *Honoring the Trust: Quality and Cost Containment in Higher Education* (Bolton, Mass.: Anker, 2003), p. 39. Massy terms the impulse to become better as "value fulfillment" and comments, "Because universities define excellence as producing as much value as they can, justifying price hikes by the high cost of excellence is circular."

[2] R.S. Kaplan and D.P. Norton, *The Strategy Focused Organization* (Boston: Harvard Business School Press, 2000).

A college or university that enjoys financial equilibrium no longer has a "structural budget deficit." Such a circumstance occurs when normal revenues (student fees and state appropriations, for example) are insufficient to meet basic expenses and maintain services at the current level. Asset sales, extraordinary gifts, hikes in endowment spending, and other one-time revenues balance the budget.

Amherst College in Massachusetts adopted a more formal statement of financial equilibrium:

- Current income must be equal to or greater than expenses. Although the concept of a balanced budget is straightforward, the model of financial equilibrium holds that budgets must be balanced without eroding financial and physical assets, as described below.

- Growth in income must be equal to or greater than growth in expenses. Even with a current balanced budget, a projection of income and expenses may reveal the strong probability of future deficits. The trend of income and expenses over time is as important as their current relationship.

- Spending from the endowment must be at or below the level necessary to preserve its real purchasing power, after adjusting for investment returns, gifts, and inflation. The practical effect of spending more than the real (inflation-adjusted) return on the endowment's investments is that future generations will subsidize present expenditures, thereby adversely affecting the financial viability of the college's programs.

- Expenditures, or contributions to reserves, for renewal and replacement of physical plant and equipment must be at or above a level that preserves their useful life. If projected budgets do not provide for the renewal and replacement of physical plant and equipment, the college will consume its physical assets and inevitably will face financial difficulties.[3]

Parts of the Budget

Budgets have three parts: (1) the operating budget, which contains current revenues and expenses; (2) the capital budget, which documents new construction and renovation, as well as the purchase of land and major equipment; and (3) the cash budget, which recognizes revenues when received and expenses when paid.[4]

Operating Budget: Object, Program, and Responsibility Center Budgets

College operating budgets can be organized in many ways, with the data presented in different formats. Three of the most prevalent are by object, program, and responsibility center. Each format answers a different expenditure question that helps

---

[3] Amherst College, "A Financial Framework Statement for Amherst College in the 1990s," *www.amherst.edu/~treasurer/financial* (accessed July 6, 2006.)

[4] Mary T. Ziebell and Don DeCosta, *Management Control in Nonprofit Organizations* (San Francisco: Harcourt Brace Jovanovich, 1991), pp. 217-219.

managers at all levels administer their budgets more effectively. Examples are shown in Exhibit 5.0 and discussed below. Notice that the total budgets are the same even though each is categorized differently.

Exhibit 5.0: Types of Operating Budgets ($000)

		This Year	Proposed Next Year
OBJECT	Salaries	$12,000	$13,000
	Benefits	$ 3,000	$ 3,500
	Operating Expenses	$ 7,000	$ 7,000
	TOTAL	**$22,000**	**$23,500**
PROGRAM	Instruction	$ 8,000	$ 8,500
	Research	$ 3,000	$ 3,000
	Institutional Support	$ 6,500	$ 6,000
	Other	$ 4,500	$ 6,000
	TOTAL	**$22,000**	**$23,500**
RESPONSIBILITY CENTER	Academic Affairs	$10,000	$10,500
	Admissions	$ 2,000	$ 2,200
	Advancement	$ 2,500	$ 2,750
	Finance	$ 4,000	$ 4,000
	Student Affairs	$ 3,500	$ 4,050
	TOTAL	**$22,000**	**$23,500**

Object Budget. The object budget answers the question: "What are we buying?" It is about controlling spending and promoting economy. Objects of expenditure include supplies, utilities, and other goods and services the institution purchases. A few budgets even list authorized numbers of desks or other equipment that employees may buy during the fiscal year. Presidents and senior administrators view the details of the object budget as concrete, understandable, and useful for monitoring expenditures, as budget allocations are broken down all the way to the administrative or academic department level.

The most significant object of expenditure usually is faculty and staff compensation, which includes salaries and benefits. Why is compensation a strategic issue? Because it accounts for 50 percent or more of total expenses, compensation forces major trade-offs in most budgets and long-range financial plans. Compensation levels affect the extent to which an institution can increase salaries and benefits while also increasing program support, maintenance, and other priorities. Compensation also is linked to institutional image, faculty and staff recruitment and retention, and to the institution's ability to hire capable personnel to implement the strategic plan. At Guilford College, having faculty and staff compensation meet certain benchmarks constituted about two-thirds of the cost of the strategic plan.

In considering compensation strategy, many officials are concerned about the growing gap between professional and undergraduate school faculty. For example, average faculty salaries in public institutions have averaged 50 percent to 100 percent higher in law and business administration than in history, sociology, and education.[5]

In addition, health-care premiums have been rising much more rapidly than salaries and wages. This compels boards and administrators to make complicated choices. For example: using a third-party insurance provider, creating a self-insurance program, or forming a consortium of colleges and other nonprofits to gain volume discounts; absorbing all or some of the premium's increase in the budget or passing it on to employees in the form of increased contributions (particularly for family coverage); and maintaining existing benefits or saving money by reducing benefits or increasing co-payments.

Program Budget. The program budget answers the question: "What are we trying to do?" The program budget is organized at object-level detail first by department and then by program or function. It allows the institution to think more holistically about its major functions rather than being limited to traditional departmental boundaries. Instruction, research, student services, and institutional support (administrative overhead) are the most significant program functions. In what is called a "program structure," each program can be further subdivided on successive levels of greater specificity — programs into subprograms, subprograms into program elements, and so on. For example, instruction as a program might be organized into doctoral, master's, undergraduate, and noncredit subprograms. The doctoral subprogram might consist of physical sciences, social sciences, and business program elements. The larger the institution or the greater need for detailed information, the greater the number of levels will be — sometimes as many as six or seven. Exhibit 5.1 contains a sample program structure from the University of North Carolina at Charlotte that has two levels, programs and subprograms.[6]

Responsibility Center Budget. This format attributes revenues and expenditures to each school and department along with a share of general institutional overhead. Responsibility center budgets attempt to decentralize management and accountability and give colleges and schools more responsibility for their own budgets. Many fear that responsibility center budgeting favors profitability over mission and program. Yet it does allow financial officers and other budget managers to compare costs and performance across the institution. That a mission-critical department requires a subsidy is not a problem; not knowing that a subsidy is needed is. Questions that are asked here are: "Who is doing the spending?" and "Which units require subsidies to survive?"[7]

Responsibility center management (RCM) is used at various private research universities. It identifies centers that earn revenue directly, such as academic departments or summer programs. Revenue is assigned to schools and colleges based on their enrollment and instruction or, in the case of revenue-earning auxiliaries, money from charges and fees. These revenue sources are supplemented by earnings from endowment and grant revenues.

---

[5] Katherine S. Mangan, "The Great Divide," *Chronicle of Higher Education* (May 30, 2003), pp. A10-A14.

[6] University of North Carolina, Charlotte, Program Classification Structure: Second Edition, Technical Report 106, *fmbld02.uncc.edu/CAFM/Docs/PRGCODES.doc* (Accessed August 27, 2006).

[7] Kent John Chabotar, "How to Develop an Effective Budget Process," in Lucie Lapovsky and Mary McKeown-Moak, *Roles and Responsibilities of the Chief Financial Officer* (San Francisco: Jossey-Bass, 1999), pp. 17-28. Other parts of the discussion on strategic budgeting are based on this chapter.

Exhibit 5.1: Sample Program Structure (University of North Carolina at Charlotte)

10 Instruction

11	General Academic Instruction (Degree-related)
12	Vocational/Technical Instruction (Degree-related)
13	Requisite Preparatory/Remedial Instruction
14	General Studies
15	Occupational-related Instruction
16	Social Roles/Interaction Instruction
17	Home and Family Life Instruction
18	Personal Interest and Leisure Instruction

20 Research

21	Institutes and Research Centers
22	Individual or Project Research

30 Public Service

31	Direct Patient Care
32	Health Care Supportive Services
33	Community Services
34	Cooperative Extension Services
35	Public Broadcasting Services

40 Academic Support

41	Library Services
42	Museums and Galleries
43	Educational Media Services
44	Academic Computing Support
45	Ancillary Support
46	Academic Administration
47	Course and Curriculum Development
48	Academic Personnel Development

50 Student Service

51	Student Service Administration
52	Social and Cultural Development
53	Counseling and Career Guidance
54	Financial Aid Administration
55	Student Auxiliary Services
56	Intercollegiate Athletics
57	Student Health/Medical Services

60 Institutional Administration

61	Executive Management
62	Financial Management and Operations
63	General Administration and Logistical Service
64	Administrative Computing Support
65	Faculty and Staff Auxiliary Services
66	Public Relations/Development
67	Student Recruitment and Admissions
68	Student Records

70 Physical Plant Operations

71	Physical Plant Administration
72	Building Maintenance
73	Custodial Services
74	Utilities
75	Landscape and Ground Maintenance
76	Major Repairs and Renovations

80 Student Financial Support

81	Scholarships
82	Fellowships

90 Independent Operations

91	Independent Operations/Institutional
92	Independent Operations/External Agencies

Responsibility centers use revenue sources to pay for salaries and benefits, operating costs, central administrative services, and for common goods that support the academic program and student life. Each responsibility center also is "taxed" by paying a participation fee that acknowledges that the center is part of the larger college or university. The fee is a form of income redistribution because the money raised is often given to responsibility centers whose revenues are less than their importance to the institution and its mission.[8]

In most institutions, the budget controlled by the chief academic officer — provost, vice president for academic affairs, academic dean — is the largest. William S. Reed, the former chief finance officer at Wellesley College in Massachusetts, argues that at least 15 critical assumptions influence the development of the academic budget. They are:

> ...the rate of inflation; the size of the student body; the rates of growth for comprehensive fees, net tuition, tuition discounting, endowment return, annual gifts, payroll, nonpersonnel expenses and computing and other capital expenses; indirect cost recovery; faculty-to-student ratio; faculty teaching load; major maintenance expenses, profitability of auxiliary enterprises; and the profitability of related activities such as a hospital or an affiliated research center.[9]

Capital Budget

In contrast to the operating budget's focus on short-term annual revenues and expenses, the capital budget attends to the institution's long-term assets. The campus master plan should be a principal determinant of the capital budget. Typically funded by a combination of gifts, debt, and transfers from operations, the capital budget pays for long-term assets such as buildings, land, and major equipment. Because most capital budgets are multiyear to correspond to the length of most construction and major renovation projects, one year of the capital budget becomes part of the annual operating budget. Capital budgets are becoming more important as colleges and universities invest huge sums in new science buildings, modern classrooms, and technology infrastructures.[10]

As Reed points out: "The costs of maintaining well-equipped laboratories and outfitting new ones are increasing faster than the rate of inflation. It is not uncommon to spend $500,000 or more to equip a new lab or create a new faculty position."[11]

Even residence and dining halls with student-centered amenities are significant capital expenses. At Bowdoin College, for example, the cost per bed for residential construction climbed from $55,000 to more than $70,000 between 1995 and 2000. Renovation costs are even higher. Figures include more than $100,000 per bed at Bowdoin for turning fraternity houses into residence halls and $175,000 per bed at Yale for its residential colleges.[12] As aging baby boomers continue to swell the ranks

---

[8] *Progress Report: Responsibility Center Management at Syracuse University* (February 14, 2005), p 2. *sumweb.syr.edu/ir/RCM%20Progress%20Report%20February%202005.pdf*. See also: Jon C. Strauss and John R. Curry, *Responsibility Center Management: Lessons from 25 Years of Decentralized Management*. (Washington D.C.: National Association of College and University Business Officers, 2002).

[9] William S. Reed, *Financial Responsibilities of Governing Boards* (Washington, D.C.: AGB/NACUBO, 2001), p. 25.

[10] Stephen T. Golding, Janet Gordon, and Arthur Gravina, "Capital Ideas for Facilities Management," *Trusteeship* (May/June 2001), pp. 20-23

[11] William S. Reed, *op cit.*, p. 77.

[12] Discussion with Yale University President Richard Levin (October 2000).

of retirees, the 1950s-era college and university campuses they attended also are aging. Physical plants that accommodated the massive enrollment expansion in the mid-20th century (especially in the public sector) demand renovation or replacement today.

An expense item with strategic significance related to the physical plant is depreciation, or a non-cash allowance for wear and tear on buildings and similar "fixed assets." Depreciation expenses, which can easily total tens of millions of dollars, must be reported on the audited financial statements of independent colleges and universities. There is no similar standard for including depreciation expense on the annual budget. Industry practice varies from including full depreciation in the annual or biennial budget, to a portion of depreciation (often linked to the amount to be spent on major maintenance), to no depreciation at all.[13] The strategic significance arises from the effect of depreciation on real and apparent financial condition and on efforts to constrain deferred maintenance.

Cash Budget

Severe cash-flow problems frequently occur even at colleges and universities with balanced budgets. There are two reasons: Cash receipts are not matched with expenses, and accrual accounting is used for financial reporting.

Meeting payroll and other short-term expenses can be challenging when cash inflows surge two or three times each year as parents pay tuition bills. An institution may have adequate receipts for the year but not during crucial periods when bills are due. Inadequate cash flow threatens the survival of small colleges almost as much as an unbalanced budget. During economic downturns, state governments encounter slower and lower tax collections that pressure the cash flows of public institutions, too.[14]

If a college's operating budget is on the accrual method, this can distort cash flows. To contribute to a positive cash flow (in which receipts exceed disbursements), the operating budget should include depreciation — a non-cash item that can accrue several million dollars in expenses that in turn can be mistaken for cash outflows. Funding depreciation by setting aside cash for the eventual replacement of buildings not only is good capital management, it also constrains this distortion of cash flow. Ordinarily, the amount to set aside initially is based on the annual depreciation charge, but this should be refined by the master plan for campus development and refurbishment.[15] The operating budget overestimates available cash in at least two ways: (1) by not including principal repayments of debt as an expense and (2) through counting pledges (for capital construction that may not be paid for years) as revenue.

Based on historical data and forecasts, a monthly or quarterly cash budget is a vital component of financial management. Such budgets should show cash inflows from operating (tuition, state appropriations), investing (dividends and interest), and

---

[13] A 2004 survey of seventeen liberal arts colleges by the author determined that only three included full depreciation in their operating or capital budgets.

[14] Tracy J. Burlock and Kent John Chabotar, *Financial Responsibilities* (Washington, D.C.: AGB, 1998), p. 10.

[15] Richard J. Meisinger, *College and University Budgeting: An introduction for Faculty and Academic Administrators,* 2nd edition (Washington, D.C.: NACUBO, 1994), p. 61.

Exhibit 5.2: Operating, Capital, and Cash Budgets ($000)

		This Year	Proposed Next Year
OPERATING	Salaries	$12,000	$13,000
	Benefits	$ 3,000	$ 3,500
	Operating expenses	$ 7,000	$ 7,000
	TOTAL	**$22,000**	**$23,500**
CAPITAL	Construction	$ 4,000	$ 3,000
	Renovation	$ 1,000	$ 2,000
	TOTAL	**$ 5,000**	**$ 5,000**
CASH (net)	Cash at start of FY	$ 3,000	$ 3,500
	Operating	$ 1,000	$ (500)
	Investing	$ 2,000	$ 2,100
	Financing	$ (2,500)	$ (2,750)
	Cash at end of FY	$ 3,500	$ 2,350
	TOTAL	**$ 3,500**	**$ 2,350**

financing (bond proceeds) activities and expenses along those same three dimensions. Debow Freed, former president of Ohio Wesleyan University, makes the important point that "Most trustees seldom see cash statements for their colleges but probably see them regularly for their businesses. They are equally important for both."[16]

Exhibit 5.2 shows the relationships among an operating budget, capital budget, and cash budget in the same institution. The cash budget is net of inflows and outflows; for example, operating cash inflows of $20,000 less outflows of $19,000 nets $1,000 shown on the exhibit.

Special Topics in Budgeting

Four topics that relate to all types of budgets are (1) pricing decisions for tuition and other fees, (2) the role of the endowment in budgeting, (3) alternative sources of revenue, and (4) adjusting historical and projected budget data for inflation.

Pricing Decisions. Pricing is among the most crucial decisions a college or university makes. When setting fees for tuition, room and board, and various activities, an institution may be fixing 50 percent of more of its total revenue.[17] What considerations should drive pricing?

1. *The direct costs and indirect overhead costs of delivering the service.* Cost will almost never equal price because colleges and universities use state aid, endowment earnings, and gifts to subsidize most services.[18] Exhibit 5.3 excerpts a cost

---

[16] DeBow Freed, "Be Vigilant on Financial Statements, *Trusteeship* (July/August 2002), pp. 15-19.

[17] See: Regina Herzlinger and Denise Nitterhouse, *Financial Accounting and Managerial Control for Nonprofit Organizations* (Cincinnati, Ohio: South-Western Educational Publishing, 1994), pp. 329-340.

[18] In 1998, the National Commission on the Cost of Higher Education pointed to the "opaque" relationship between college costs and prices, and urged institutions to help the public understand the difference. See: *Straight Talk about College Costs and Prices* (Phoenix: American Council on Education/ Oryx Press, 1998), pp. 12-14.

Exhibit 5.3: Sample Cost Study

Research indicates that per credit hour, nontraditional Center for Continuing Education (CCE) adult students actually provide a higher contribution margin than the other categories of student. The traditional on-campus student population has the next highest contribution margin, followed by traditional off-campus, study-abroad, and finally, high school students in the Early College at Guilford (ECG).

The results of this analysis are included in the summary shown below. In terms of dollar amount, the traditional residential student contributed the greatest margin with $6,144 (revenue less direct costs and instructional costs). In terms of percentage, the CCE student contributed the highest percentage (49 percent). The analysis also showed that the allocated costs (operation and maintenance, depreciation, and so forth) were the greatest for the traditional residential student ($8,029) and the least for the CCE student ($2,654). Thus, based on this study, the category with the highest net margin (revenue less direct, instructional, and allocated costs) is the CCE student. [Note: The net contribution numbers are all negative because tuition and fees generate only approximately two-thirds of the college's total revenue.]

	Traditional students (in residence) with 15.7 credit hours	Traditional students (commuting) with 15.7 credit hours	CCE students with 10.3 credit hours	Early College students with 14.8 credit hours
Gross revenue per student	$23,680	$17,900	$4,384	$5,600
Less: Direct costs (financial aid)	($13,614)	($11,363)	($292)	($1,185)
Less: Instructional costs	($3,922)	($3,922)	($1,955)	($3,697)
Gross contribution margin	**$6,144**	**$2,616**	**$2,136**	**$718**
Less: Allocated costs	($8,029)	($5,948)	($2,654)	($8,717)
Net contribution margin	**($1,885)**	**($3,333)**	**($518)**	**($7,999)**
Gross margin contribution percentage	26%	15%	49%	13%
Net contribution margin percentage	-8%	-19%	-12%	-143%
Gross contribution margin per credit hour	$196	$83	$104	$24
Net contribution margin per credit hour	($60)	($106)	($25)	($270)

study from Guilford College that estimated the costs of traditional, adult, and early college high school student programs, along with their respective contributions to financial equilibrium.

2. *The expected net revenue (after deducting such costs as financial aid) given volume and price.* Although higher prices often yield lower volume, this has not occurred in higher education where the demand for admission to the most expensive, elite schools continues to far exceed the supply of openings.

3. *How aggressive the institution chooses to be in order to fund educational quality and to "protect the product."* Quality at elite colleges seems inextricably linked with spending, both

perceptually and statistically. Quality-protection advocates argue for "pushing the envelope" on revenues (higher tuition and/or endowment spending) to support academic and social aspirations as well as the institution's competitive position against wealthier rivals.

4. *The pricing philosophy of the organizational units.* Graduate, undergraduate, and adult-education programs may charge different prices per semester, course, or credit hour. Some units, such as the bookstore and dining service, may be profit centers from which the institution expects net income. Others may be expense centers that lose money (many parts of the academic program) or break even.

5. *In public institutions, the extent to which state appropriations and financial need influence tuition prices.* As states assume smaller shares of the budgets of public colleges and universities, pricing decisions have become more sensitive in terms of the effects on enrollment. Financial-aid policy also has gained importance. Pricing decisions often are complicated by many variables — for example, in-state and out-of-state tuition levels, percentage caps and targets for out-of-state students, and how much of a price increase should be in tuition and how much in fees (the latter more likely to be retained by the institution).

6. *The institution's philosophy about affordability and access.* Many less selective independent colleges are struggling with contrasting strategies: High tuition implies top quality; low tuition signals affordability.

A dilemma boards and administrators face is how to set the prices of student fees in relation to institutional financial aid. Some institutions set tuition high but also award substantial amounts of need-based financial aid. This "high tuition/high aid" model assumes that higher income students will pay more in tuition and allow the institution to focus its financial-aid dollars on grants for low-income students. Highly selective institutions have an easier time making this model work because they have the prestige to attract many high-income students who also are academically well qualified.

Other colleges and universities constrain both tuition and financial aid, adopting a "low tuition/low aid" model. In fact, a few less-selective institutions have even cut their tuition to become "low tuition/low aid" institutions. Wells College in New York, Wesleyan College in North Carolina, and Muskingum College in Ohio slashed tuition for entering students by as much as 30 percent during the late 1990s. The results varied, but each institution experienced more applications, higher enrollments, and improved test scores (at least in the short term) and awarded less financial aid.[19] Exhibit 5.4 summarizes the advantages and limitations of each model.[20]

An emerging variation on the "high tuition/high aid model" relates to the relative proportions of financial aid based on need versus merit. "Merit" generally pertains to a student's academic qualifications, but it increasingly describes a

---

[19] R.G. Ehrenberg, *Tuition Rising* (Cambridge, Mass.: Harvard University Press, 2000), p. 83.

[20] See also: Lucie Lapovsky, "What You Need to Know about Enrollment Management" in Lucie Lapovsky and Mary P. McKeown-Moak (eds.), *Roles and Responsibilities of the Chief Financial Officer* (San Francisco: Jossey-Bass, 1999), pp. 5-15.

Exhibit 5.4: Comparative Analysis of Pricing Models

	Advantages	Limitations
High Tuition/ High Aid	Price is closer to actual cost of education because all students are subsidized regardless of need.	Subsidy should be broadened through low tuition rather than targeted only at needy students.
	Provides more tuition revenue to use on financial aid for needy students.	Less likely to enroll high-income and low-need students without preferential packaging.
	High "sticker price" may be associated with higher quality.	High "sticker price" may lead to sticker shock and fewer applications.
		Targeting aid and identifying eligible students is a complex undertaking.
Low Tuition/ Low Aid	More equitable subsidization of all students.	Increases subsidy regardless of ability to pay.
	Short-term publicity and boost in applications.	Long-term effects on applications vary with institution.
	Appears more affordable, especially to first-time college applicants.	Low price may be associated with lower quality.
		Academic reputation and career prospects are more important in college choice than cost or aid.

student's overall suitability, which includes the family's ability to pay. Less selective schools engage in "preferential packaging," in which "merit" grant aid is used to enroll high-income, academically desirable students who ordinarily would qualify for more-selective schools but who would receive little or no need-based aid. The ability to enroll these students often means the difference between a balanced and an unbalanced budget.

Some public institutions have become better able to influence or set tuition levels, often in exchange for less state support. Setting out-of-state tuition more competitively, or closer to the real cost, also has become more common, especially for selective public institutions and those in states with enrollment capacity issues. Some institutions are charging differential tuition by programs to reflect their real costs, especially for graduate and professional programs.

Role of the Endowment. The board should diversify its investments enough to provide a total return sufficient to operate the institution and grow the endowment while avoiding dangerous speculation. Annual endowment spending — typically expressed as a percentage of the current or lagging average of the endowment's market value — must preserve the endowment's purchasing power while funding the institution's expressed priorities. One rule of thumb is that the yearly total return of the endowment in income and gains must be equal to or greater than spending for the budget plus inflation. Thus, a college with a 10 percent total return that spent the equivalent of 5 percent of the endowment market value when inflation is 3 percent would meet this test.

Independent colleges and universities always have considered their endowments to be a principal source of stability and consistent support. This was particularly true when institutions invested endowments mostly in certificates of deposit, treasury bills, and other fixed-rate instruments with relatively low yields but high predictability. Nevertheless, with the emergence of a total-return philosophy that allows institutions to spend capital gains as well as income, endowment proportions have changed noticeably toward common stocks, private equity, venture capital, and real estate, all of which have greater potential for long-term appreciation. Moreover, such concentration away from fixed income was spectacularly rewarded in the 1990s with annual returns for some portfolios that exceeded 20 percent and, for venture capital alone, over 50 percent in some years.[21]

Public universities also have become more interested in endowments, operating in partnership with affiliated foundations that protect the income flow from the many vagaries of legislative appropriation. Many foundations grew out of well-known athletics booster clubs. Multibillion-dollar endowments at Michigan, Texas, Virginia, and other flagship universities provided dramatic incentives for other public institutions to intensify fund-raising and develop foundations.

Fundamental Concepts. The endowment supports the budget mainly by distributing investment income and capital appreciation to various funds for spending during the fiscal year. Some funds are restricted by a donor (an individual, foundation, or the state government) to specific purposes such as financial aid or faculty research. Others are unrestricted and spendable for any purpose subject to institutional budgeting practices. On occasion, the board internally may designate unrestricted funds for particular purposes, such as technology or scholarships for a specific term, years, or indefinitely.

The original gift and subsequent gifts to a "true" endowment fund (also known as the "corpus") may never be spent; the income and appreciation may be spent. Usually funded by budget surpluses or gifts, a "quasi-endowment" (also known as "board designated endowment") may have its corpus spent as well as any income and appreciation. Unrestricted quasi-endowment often constitutes a financial reserve for the institution. Think of the resulting table to clarify the relationship among these fundamental concepts:

	Restricted	Unrestricted
True	1	2
Quasi	3	4

Colleges and universities should know not only the market value of the total endowment but also how much is contained within each category. For example, two institutions might have $50 million endowments. Of the $50 million total endowment, Institution A has less than $200,000 left in unrestricted quasi-endowment due to years of using it to cover budget deficits. Institution B has half of its $50 million in unrestricted quasi-endowment that suggests much greater flexibility to cope with an unexpected budget shortfall or fund a strategic opportunity. Such broader perspectives are lost when only the total amount of an endowment is considered.

The amount of money available for such purposes depends on the institution's endowment spending formula. For example, it is common for institutions to use

---

[21] Edward Wyatt, "College Endowments Learn to Live with Risk," *New York Times* (November 19, 2000).

5 percent of a 12-quarter or three-year lagging average of endowment market values.[22] The lagging average is used to avoid sudden fluctuations in endowment support due to market conditions and has the effect of constraining spending in "boom" years and boosting spending in "bust" years.

Budget Support. The operating budget relies on endowment earnings for a portion of its revenues. A 2003 report stated that the California Institute of Technology relied on its endowment for 20 percent of its operating budget, while tuition revenue accounted for only 4 percent. That same report claimed that endowment earnings funded about 40 percent of the budget at Claremont McKenna College.[23] When David Swenson of Yale University examined this issue among highly endowed private research universities, he discovered that Harvard, Princeton, and Yale relied on endowment for about 25 percent of the budget. When other universities were grouped into quartiles by endowment size, the proportions ranged from 4 percent to 17 percent of the budget, with higher proportions strongly correlated with higher endowment market values.[24]

Endowment gains and income also can be included in the capital budget for new construction and renovation — frequently to pay debt service. Principal amounts of funds functioning as endowment (or quasi-endowment) can be allocated to the capital budget for building projects.

Spending Formula. For both the capital and operating budgets, endowment spending must be limited to the long-term spending formula. Wellesley College, for example, had a spending formula of 6 percent that was divided into about 4.5 percent for operations and 1.5 percent for capital. Institutions often are tempted to exceed the spending formula for projects that are deemed critical to admissions or academic programs, even as soliciting new gifts or taking on new debt might be more prudent options. The market downturn from 2000-03 led institutions such as Middlebury (Vermont) and Oberlin (Ohio) colleges to draw more from endowment than usual. Dartmouth College in New Hampshire took a different approach and made up its shortfall by cutting the budget.[25] Nationally, the *2005 NACUBO Endowment Study* revealed that market gains had led to larger endowments and enabled the average spending rate in 2004-05 to drop to 4.7 percent compared with 5 percent in 2003-04. The spending rate had been increasing the four previous fiscal years.[26]

Exhibit 5.5 depicts two ways that the endowment influences budgeting; (1) the often-overlooked use of quasi-endowment that exceeds the spending formula and (2) the difference between distribution and actual spending. In the exhibit, the spending formula "distributed" and the amount of distribution "spent" differ not

---

[22] Technically, what is called a "spending formula" is really a "distribution formula" since the 5 percent or other "spending" rate dictates how much is distributed to endowment funds and not how much is actually spent.

[23] John Pulley, "Another Downer of a Year in College Endowments," *Chronicle of Higher Education* (January 24, 2003), pp. A23-A27.

[24] David F. Swensen, *Pioneering Portfolio Management* (New York: The Free Press, 2000), pp. 22-23.

[25] Ben Gose, "Prudent Management or Outright Greed? Critics Ask How Big Endowments Should Be" *Chronicle of Higher Education* (May 28, 2004), p. B-10.

[26] Mimi Lord, *Trends and Issues: Highlights of the 2005 NACUBO Endowment Study* (TIAA-CREF Institute, 2006), p. 9 and *Trends and Issues: Highlights of the 2004 NACUBO Endowment Study* (TIAA-CREF Institute, 2005), p 2.

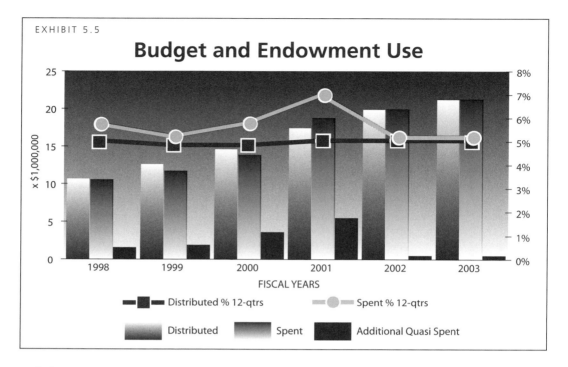

EXHIBIT 5.5

Budget and Endowment Use

FISCAL YEARS

Distributed % 12-qtrs   Spent % 12-qtrs

Distributed   Spent   Additional Quasi Spent

only because it is usually impossible to spend all of the annual distribution but also because institutions periodically tap the unspent distributions from prior years. For example, a university may not be able to find students who meet the terms of restricted scholarships or faculty members who qualify for endowed professorships in specific disciplines in one year but can find them the next year. Thus, the institution may be able to spend $16 million of the $17 million annual distribution for FY 2000-01 plus $2 million left over from prior years, which sums to $18 million in distributions spent for FY 2000-01. Adding $5 million spent from quasi-endowment means that total spending from endowment was $23 million that year. While the distribution rate that year was 5 percent, total spending (including the use of quasi-endowment, which would not be counted in the distribution rate) was 7 percent.

What is the right proportion of endowment support for the budget? Aside from aiming for a 5 percent distribution rate, should officials also establish a target percentage of the budget to be funded by endowment gains and income? There is no standard proportion for all institutions because of such factors as the size of the budget and endowment (in both absolute and relative terms), market conditions, and investment philosophy and goals. Nevertheless, the proportion of the budget funded by the endowment might be among the strategic indicators regularly reported to the board.

Alternative Sources of Revenue. A 2003 report from the American Council on Education provides useful guidance on alternative revenue streams for colleges. The report investigated these alternatives in eight domains:

· *Instruction*, including online programming and niche-oriented non-degree programming.

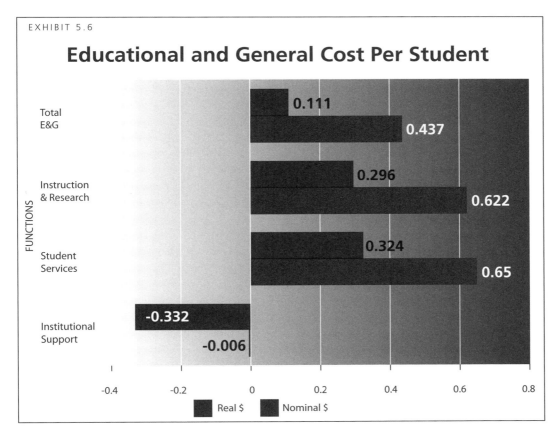

EXHIBIT 5.6

Educational and General Cost Per Student

Research and analysis, including technology-transfer initiatives, business incubators, and e-commerce initiatives.

· *Pricing,* including differential pricing and user fees.

· *Financial decision making and management,* including venture capital investment as well as participation in arbitrage and options markets.

· *Human resources,* including compensation incentives for entrepreneurship and retirement or rehiring incentives for faculty.

· *Franchising, licensing, sponsorship, and partnering arrangements with third parties,* including logo-bearing clothing, tours and camps, and event sponsorships.

· *Auxiliary enterprises, facilities, and real estate,* including debit cards, facility rentals, and alumni services.

· *Development,* including appeals to donors abroad and other efforts.[27]

Adjusting for Inflation. Analyzing revenues and expenses in nominal dollars (out-of-pocket) as well as constant (inflation-adjusted) dollars can be interesting and informative. For example, an inflation analysis is essential to understand the

[27] James C. Hearn, *Diversifying Campus Revenue Streams: Opportunities and Risks* (Washington, D.C.: American Council on Education, 2003).

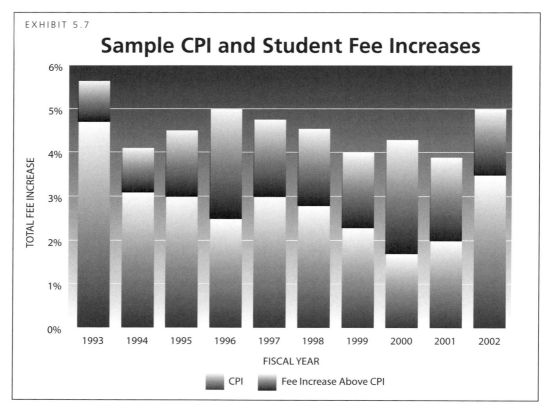

EXHIBIT 5.7

Sample CPI and Student Fee Increases

TOTAL FEE INCREASE

FISCAL YEAR

CPI   Fee Increase Above CPI

real returns on the endowment. A nominal return of 12 percent on a portfolio may shrink to 9 percent after inflation is considered, and the differences expand with the compounding of a longitudinal analysis. Huge apparent increases in the budget may become real decreases when inflation is added to the equation. Exhibit 5.6 depicts how educational and general (E&G) costs per student seemed to skyrocket over ten years when expressed in nominal dollars — for example, instruction and research by 62 percent. Adjusting for inflation, however, slowed these increases by half and actually reduced real per-student costs for institutional support by one-third.

Consumer Price Index. Some budget items are related to the growth in the Consumer Price Index (CPI), a measure familiar to students and parents as well as trustees. For example, the 1.6 percent increase in CPI for the year ending October 31, 2002, could be a reference point in preparing a proposed budget for FY 2003-04. An institution might target student-fee growth at one-and-one-half to two percentage points above the CPI rise to reflect its own costs. As Exhibit 5.7 shows, much of the annual increase in tuition and fees often is consumed by just trying to keep up with inflation.

Higher Education Price Index. As measured by the Higher Education Price Index (HEPI), U.S. college costs have climbed more rapidly than consumer prices. For example, between 1980 and 2000, consumer prices measured by the CPI increased about 118 percent, while HEPI rose 154 percent.[28] Why? Colleges pay salaries, build

---

[28] Kent Halstead, *Inflation Measures for Schools, Colleges, & Libraries* (Arlington, Va.: Research Associates, 2001), pp. 4-5. See also: John Griswold, "What's the Best Yardstick to Measure Inflation?" *Trusteeship* 14, no. 4 (July/August 2006), p. 24

roads, purchase laboratory equipment, and incur other expenses that the CPI does not recognize. Higher education is labor-intensive; compensation accounts for half or more of most budgets and grows at one to two percentage points above consumer inflation. And colleges and universities must comply with federal regulations on such matters as hazardous waste disposal, nondiscrimination, student aid, and other matters.

Escalating costs reflect not only higher prices but also a higher volume of activity, such as hiring more faculty, expanding residential life, and paying more debt service.

Budget Targets

All budgets should have targets in order to facilitate decision making and provide a theory for the budget that is transparent to everyone. Some targets arise from performance indicators in the strategic plan. Others represent mandates from the president, the board, the state legislature, and various regulators. Targets can be absolute (the university will lower its tuition discount to 25 percent) or comparative (the tuition discount will be at the midpoint of a peer group). One national liberal arts college relied on institutional and comparative indicators that were at first defined piecemeal. The board and administration gradually refined the indicators over a 25-year period, as shown in Exhibit 5.8.

The current year's budget frequently is the most significant influence on next year's budget. Budgeting tends to be incremental, adding to and subtracting from an existing budget rather than springing from a more comprehensive, zero-based approach.

Budget managers should consult widely to collect as much information and advice as possible on budget resources, priorities, new programs, and other "budget drivers." Enrollment ceilings, hiring controls, salary savings targets, and midyear reductions may limit budget discretion. Trustees can serve as a reality check on budget assumptions by offering observations from community, state, and corporate perspectives.

Exhibit 5.8: Sample Budget Targets

Total budget	balanced, with shifting emphasis toward academic program and residential life and away from institutional support
Tuition and fees	median of the comparison group
Financial aid	need-blind, spending from 12.5 percent to 14 percent of budget on 36 percent to 40 percent of students
Endowment spending	4.75 percent long-term of 12-quarter lagging average of market value
Faculty salaries	60th percentile within comparison group
Administrative and support staff salaries	50th percentile of relevant labor markets
Employee benefits	50th percentile of comparison group
Major maintenance and capital projects	$3 million adjusted for inflation
Academic program	achievement of 10.5 to 1 student-to-faculty ratio
Information technology	four-year replacement cycle for desktop computers
Athletics	median spending among athletic conference schools within four years

In public institutions, the budget process must comport with state requirements. Budgets may be formula-driven by square footage or the numbers of faculty and students. Cooperation with the state is essential to secure adequate government appropriations or to issue bonds.

What Constitutes a Strategic Budget?

Strategic budgeting is defined by its explicit linkages to the institution's strategic plan. A strategic budget funds and implements the institution's mission, vision, and core values, and the budget process is organized around the institution's strategic direction and its short-term initiatives. In approving the institution's budget, the board is endorsing a set of priorities for the year — and beyond. It also is allocating financial, capital, and human assets to those ends. Conversely, a budget that is not strategic responds to short-term needs and crises and is developed one year at a time without much historical perspective or extensive future projections.

Characteristics. What signals a truly strategic budget? A truly strategic budget does the following:

- consistently refers to the mission and values of the institution as well as the long-range financial plan to justify expected revenues and expenses;

- synchronizes budgeted revenues and expenses with board investment policies and long-term outlook for the endowment and foundation;

- shows the assumptions and risks underlying budget recommendations;

- justifies increases in student fees by price inflation and new or expanded program initiatives and facilities;

- relates the operating budget to the capital and cash budgets;

- clearly distinguishes between continuing and one-time revenues and expenses;

- sets limits on the number of positions that may be on the payroll through broadly defined categories linked to the strategic plan (for example, by schools or divisions rather than specific departments);

- discloses the full impact of new positions not just in terms of pay and benefits but start-up funds, computers, office space, and staff support;

- links the major maintenance budget to the campus master plan, amount of deferred maintenance, and major functions such as safety, building infrastructure, aesthetics, and program improvement;

- provides for contingency funds either explicitly or by creating reserves through not budgeting vacancy savings, assuming lower than expected enrollment, and basing utility budgets on extreme weather conditions; and

- explains the comparative data and benchmarks used in developing the budget.

Financial Planning Models

Financial planning models forecast revenues and expenses five years or more to detect future implications of current budgets. They reveal how even small percentage increases compound quickly over time. The model can cover the entire budget or key parts to address such specific issues as the following:

- effects on total compensation of faculty appointment and promotion rates;

- endowment growth given varying rates of return on investment and new gifts;

- long-term costs of new program initiatives or long-term savings for program elimination;

- total financial-aid costs and discount rates at varying rates of increase in tuition and fees; and

- effects on tuition and fees if state appropriations decline and a balanced budget must be maintained.

The model can confirm or discourage the institution's ambitions before scarce resources are committed. Assumptions for forecasting must be clear and convincing and take into account factors such as inflation, annual fund and capital campaign expectations, levels of state appropriations, and formula funding. An effective model is simple and complete so that decision makers can understand and control the predictability of the model's outputs. It is adaptable to the data needs of the decision maker, and its terms are easy to communicate to a wide range of constituencies.[29]

A financial planning model has six standard components:

1. **Units of analysis.** The model identifies the units of analysis — the functions or other items to be forecast. Revenues by source and expenditures by function and line item are most common. Functional expenses include instruction, academic support (library), student services (admissions, athletics, student affairs), institutional support (president, deans, and vice presidents), and auxiliary enterprises (dining services, bookstore, nonacademic summer programs). Line items included are salaries and benefits, purchased services (travel, consultants, audit, and legal fees), utilities, and depreciation.

2. **Forecast period.** This is the period for which the forecast is needed, usually expressed in years. Most financial plans do not project much beyond five years because longer periods make forecasts less reliable. The forecast usually proceeds from a prior baseline period of one or two years for which audited results are known and the current fiscal year.

   William Massy, the former Stanford University finance officer, divides the forecast period into two segments,:

   The equilibrium period is the last year of the planning period. The organizational intent is to achieve "financial equilibrium" by that year, including

---

[29] Joe B. Wyatt, James C. Emery, and Carolyn P. Landis *et al.*, eds., *Financial Planning Models: Concepts and Case Studies in Colleges and Universities* (Princeton, N.J.: EDUCOM, 1979), pp. 36-38.

a balanced budget with no hidden liabilities. Growth rates of income and expense are determined on the basis of long-term economic considerations. For example, salaries might be expected to grow at 1 percent over inflation based on productivity growth in the economy, while tuition may grow by 1.25 percent over inflation based on the expected growth of family income. Equilibrium is represented by only one year in the model, but it represents the indefinite future.

The transition period describes the transition from the current budget to the desired equilibrium period. It may be any length, but three to five years seems appropriate. Growth-rate assumptions during transition are based on short-run factors. For example, one might decide to move up a few places in the tuition rankings and forecast that this will require an extra 3 percent growth per year for three years. Likewise, restoring salary shortfalls might require an extra 1.5 percent growth per year, or working off a deferred maintenance backlog might require an addition of $1 million a year to the base.

For Massy, thinking separately about the transition and equilibrium periods (that is, the difference between short-run and long-run issues) represents the essence of strategic finance.[30]

3. **Assumptions.** These are the bases on which the forecasts are made. Some are percentages based on historical data; others are historical percentages adjusted for new revenues and expenses (for example, salaries projected at 5 percent, rather than the historical 4 percent, to account for increased competition). Percentages also can be projected from expected rates of inflation; for example, salaries might be projected at one percentage point above 3 percent inflation. Assumptions also can be concrete plans with fluctuating rates of increase or decrease, such as revenues reflecting a capital campaign plan and expenses reflecting costs of new construction and utilities.

4. **Trends.** The compounded rates of total increase or decrease in each unit of analysis are calculated. For example, based on annual increases of 4 percent over five years, the compound rate is 27.6 percent. Exhibit 5.9 shows sample results of a financial planning model in which total expenses and revenues are depicted as a graph with specific sources and uses of funds detailed below. Note that the trend line crosses in the last year of the analysis as expenses begin to exceed revenues.

5. **Sensitivity analysis.** What might be done to rebalance revenues and expenses? Small changes in any of the model's assumptions can have significant effects. For example, at one college every 1 percent increase or decrease in the comprehensive student fee yielded $175,000 after the financial-aid discount. Exhibit 5.10 shows a more complete analysis.

6. **Scenarios.** No strategic plan or budget is permanent. Trustees, presidents, and others should anticipate change by developing alternative scenarios of revenues, expenses, and net income. It is impossible to fix a response in every situation. For example, a response to a forced reduction in student fees would

---

[30] Comments from William Massy to Kent Chabotar (2003).

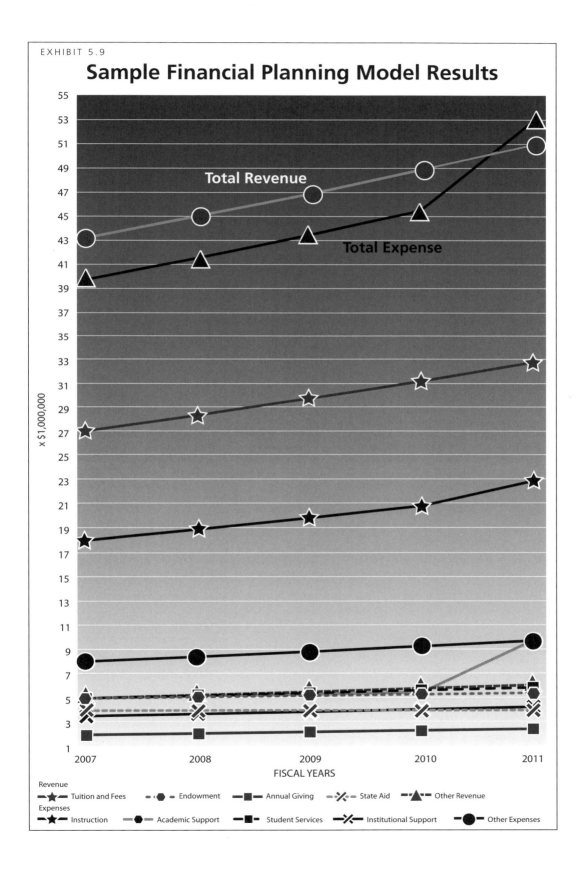

EXHIBIT 5.9

Sample Financial Planning Model Results

x $1,000,000

Total Revenue

Total Expense

FISCAL YEARS

Revenue
★ Tuition and Fees   ● Endowment   ■ Annual Giving   ✕ State Aid   ▲ Other Revenue

Expenses
★ Instruction   ● Academic Support   ■ Student Services   ✕ Institutional Support   ● Other Expenses

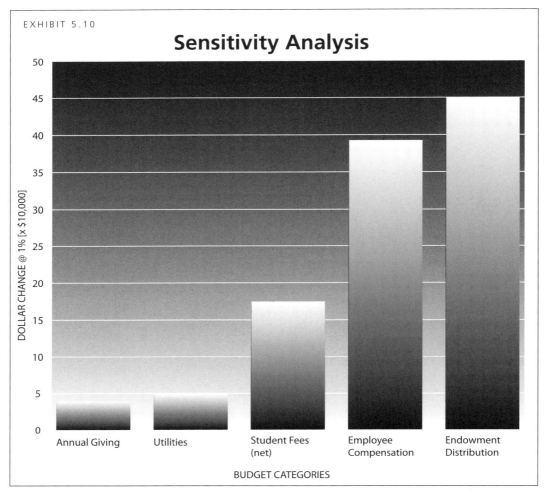

EXHIBIT 5.10

Sensitivity Analysis

depend on whether it was due to price competition or an economic recession. In the former case, the institution would have more flexibility in using endowment to bridge the gap than if a recession impaired families' ability to pay and the institution's endowment market value, while also increasing the institution's financial-aid obligations.

It is useful to create "best case" and "worst case" scenarios. For example, forecasting what would occur after a precipitous drop in financial markets and annual giving during a period of high inflation can be useful. Each scenario also needs to define an institutional response to such events.

The reliability of the model should be checked going back three to five years — pretending that actual revenues and expenses today are unknown. Which forecasting assumption would have most accurately predicted net tuition revenue, appropriations, annual giving, and other budget items? Results of this analysis can be used to fine-tune the model going forward.

One fundamental priority of a college or university budget is to link with the strategic plan and long-range financial plan. How does the budget — whether expressed in objects of expenditure or responsibility centers — implement the plan's mission and vision as well as financing? A second priority is for the budget to contribute to institutional "financial equilibrium." Financial equilibrium demands more than a balanced budget. It also requires that the budget be balanced by setting prices that maintain enrollment and diversity, preserving such resources as the endowment, and allowing adequate investment in such areas as employee compensation and building maintenance — all indicators of a well-managed and strategically focused institution.

CHAPTER 6

The Budgeting Process

Process matters in higher education. Faculty, staff, and others are accustomed to being involved in decisions ranging from curriculum to construction. Until a decade or so ago, budgeting was seen as a technical exercise consisting of completing worksheets and waiting for allocations from the finance office. But with much more competition for scarce resources and the recognition that budgets often dictate priorities more effectively than strategic plans, the importance of the budgeting process has risen markedly.

What factors shape the budget process at a college or university? Author Richard Meisinger, assistant dean for planning and new initiatives at the University of Washington's School of Medicine, lists the following:

- **Institutional character** — in terms of history, mission, geographic location, image, and control. A budgeting process at a large public university, for example, will have more controls outside of the institution than a private liberal arts college. In public institutions, budgets may be driven by formulas — for the number of faculty and students or by square footage. Budget discretion may be limited by enrollment ceilings, hiring freezes, salary savings targets, and midyear reductions.

- **Trust** — with the relationships among individuals and constituencies at the institution and with governments, foundations, and other supporters. Trust promotes better communication and a willingness to share power.

- **Openness with information** — the extent to which data are shared throughout the institution and decision-making processes are transparent. At Guilford College, for example, the campus intranet routinely publishes plans, budgets, consulting reports, and digests of the meetings of the senior staff and trustees.

- **Decision-making authority** — the levels at which major decisions ordinarily are made. Even though conventional wisdom is that most decisions should be made "where the action is" at lower levels, the reality is that the senior administration — and in the case of public institutions, the state government — often makes most of the major decisions. A budget process must take into account the degree of centralization of decision-making authority if increased involvement is sought.[1]

This chapter examines the range of processes available to develop the annual budget, especially in the context of a strategic plan. It offers guidelines for adopting an efficient and, insofar as possible, inclusive approach to budgeting as well as suggestions for the roles of the president, board, chief financial officer, and others.

---

[1] Richard J. Meisinger, ed., *College and University Budgeting,* 2nd ed. (Washington, D.C.: NACUBO, 1994), pp. 51-59.

Approaches to Process

Many chief finance officers are comfortable with a "top down" approach in which the administration and board prepare the budget. Yet a campus community is more likely to understand and accept a budget that its members have helped develop. By introducing terms and concepts of financial management, a budgeting process can be experienced as an educational process as well. The results are that the rationale for priorities may become clearer, and the budget may reflect campus realities more accurately. Critics of any final budget are inevitable, but the predominant view likely will be that the budget is fair if the process was fair.

From membership on a campuswide budget committee to attendance at open meetings, faculty and others will have many chances to comment on and influence the process. To the extent that their comments change the budget, participants will feel satisfied and empowered. Communications over a budget also may have unintended consequences such as encouraging people from different parts of the campus to meet and work together, possibly for the first time. A budget prepared hierarchically often filters out unpleasant realities, as recommendations and analyses are summarized (and often sanitized) for successively higher levels of authority.

Three approaches may engage the community in the budgeting process:

· An *informational approach* provides periodic updates to faculty and staff about the process and decisions. The administration announces data about probable revenues

Exhibit 6.0: Participatory Budgeting Worksheet

	YES	NO
1. Do not confuse true participatory budgeting with informational or consultative budgeting.	☐	☐
2. Use a budget committee, with someone other than the CFO as chair.	☐	☐
3. Set clear expectations and limits at the start, especially priorities and authority of the chief executive and trustees.	☐	☐
4. Start early and allow more time.	☐	☐
5. Provide adequate staff and timely data.	☐	☐
6. Schedule community meetings during the process, after checking open meeting laws and union contracts.	☐	☐
7. Involve trustees early and often.	☐	☐
8. Appoint overlapping membership between the budget committee and other governance bodies.	☐	☐
9. Develop budget on two tracks: bottom-up for departmental requests and top-down for major budget drivers such as fees and endowment spending.	☐	☐
10. Implement participation slowly and gradually. Allow the culture to adapt to a new process.	☐	☐
11. Reflect on the process annually and incorporate changes to make the process more effective and efficient.	☐	☐
12. Link the budget to the organization's strategic plan.	☐	☐

and budget priorities through memoranda and regular meetings but does not actively solicit feedback.

- Others use a *consultative approach* in which opinions about the budget are actively sought and debated. The chief executive may ask for input at a faculty meeting or student government conference or from individuals. Their ideas sometimes alter decisions about various budget allocations.

- In the most *participative approach*, faculty and staff draft the budget, typically by forming a committee and holding hearings, and recommend the budget to the president and trustees (and in a public institution, eventually to the governor and legislature). Exhibit 6.0 presents the principles of a participative budgeting process.[2]

Any of these approaches, including the participative, may be used at the department or division level. They do not necessarily have to be implemented campuswide. For example, a dean of engineering might involve faculty and staff throughout the school in participative budgeting even if the university follows an informational or consultative approach. Clearly, this is not ideal, but a difference in decision-making styles should not preclude involvement in the budget process in a department that desires it.

Challenges of Increased Participation

Colleges and universities that seek to become more inclusive in their budget decision-making processes will need to consider several issues. The process becomes more time-consuming and complex as more individuals become involved. The need to pay attention to the strategic plan becomes essential to maintain a strategy-focused institution. Some budget decisions are technical and require specialized expertise. Finally, at some point, debate and analysis must stop and the budget be completed if the institution is to operate and serve its strategic and operational priorities.

1. **Time and complexity.** Moving from the informational model to the participative model, the process obviously becomes more open and moves more slowly. It takes time to prepare communications materials for the campus, organize meetings and other vehicles to obtain reactions, and compile responses to questions and suggestions. A committee needs more time than an individual to make decisions. Participative budgeting also requires more steps than does a top-down budget in terms of training, meetings, and budget hearings. A sample calendar for a campuswide budget committee is included in Exhibit 6.1.

    Becoming more participative also increases the risks of controversy, leaks of sensitive information and tentative decisions, and of an unwieldy process. This can result in a budget that may be unacceptable to the administration.

---

[2] Kent John Chabotar, "Managing Participative Budgeting in Higher Education," *Change* (September/October 1995), pp. 21-29.

Exhibit 6.1: Sample Budget Meeting Schedule

Date	Time	Location	Purpose
Tu Sep 6	3:30-5 pm	Chamberlain Room	Orientation for new committee members
Th Sep 8	3:30-5 pm	Chamberlain Room	First regular meeting; Discuss president's budget letter and budget material
Tu Sep 27	1-2 pm	Boren Lounge	CFO hosts open meeting with campus budget managers to discuss budget preparation for FY 2006-07
Th Sep 29	3:30-5 pm	Elliot-Lyman Room	Regular committee meeting to discuss major budget variables such as fees, enrollment, salaries and wages; president's charge to committee
Th Oct 6	3:30-5 pm	Chamberlain Room	Regular meeting to review enrollment and tuition and fee analysis from admissions and institutional research
We Oct 12	3:30-5 pm	Chamberlain Room	Regular meeting to review analysis of staff compensation from human resources.
Oct 15-23			**FALL BREAK**
Th Oct 27	3:30-5 pm	Elliot-Lyman Room	Regular meeting to discuss departmental request summaries and major maintenance; prepare for community forum.
Fr Oct 28	4-5 pm	JFK Center	Committee hosts community forum to discuss FY 2006-07 budget.
Mo Nov 7	3:30-5 pm	Chamberlain Room	Regular meeting to discuss Academic Affairs budget
Fr Nov 11	3:30-5 pm	Chamberlain Room	Regular meeting to discuss Student Affairs budget
We Nov 16	3:30-5 pm	Elliot-Lyman Room	Regular meeting to discuss Development targets and budget
Tu Nov 22	3:30-5 pm	Elliot-Lyman Room	Regular meeting to discuss Finance and Administration budget
Th Dec 1	10-11 am	Fessenden Room	Conference Call between Budget Committee and Finance Committee of Board of Trustees
We Dec 14	8:30-12 noon	Elliot-Lyman Room	Extended meeting to discuss budget recommendations
Fr Dec 16	8:30-12 noon	Elliot-Lyman Room	Extended meeting to discuss budget recommendations (if needed)
Dec 17-Jan 9			**WINTER BREAK**
Tu Jan 17	3:30-5 pm	Chamberlain Room	Check-in meeting to finalize budget recommendations
We Jan 18	8:30 am-5 pm	Fessenden Room	Conference Calls between Treasurer and Budget Committee Chair with Board Committees (finance, academic affairs, facilities, admissions)
Mo Jan 23	4-5 pm	JFK Center	Committee hosts community forum to discuss FY 2006-07 budget.
We Jan 25			Recommended budget sent to President
Mo Feb 6			Recommended budget send to Board of Trustees
Sa Feb 25			Budget approved by Board of Trustees

Usually, participation may be increased incrementally over a year or two. For example, the first year may involve more administrative direction and fewer all-campus meetings than subsequent years will. As it gains more experience, the committee may want to "jump start" the process by compiling early forecasts in the spring before the formal start of budget development in the fall.

2. **Strategic context.** A budget needs a context to be both realistic and comprehensible — especially in a participative process. Part of that context is the institution's mission and strategic plan. After all, the budget should reflect priorities set forth in the plan. It is harder to claim that instruction is a top priority when its budget allocation, in dollars or in percentage of total, shows a declining trend.

3. **Technical decisions.** The campuswide budget committee can struggle to make good decisions in areas in which its members may require additional expertise — usually technology issues and enrollment projections — especially where circumstances have changed since adoption of the strategic plan. Referring technology requests only to the budget committee risks making expensive decisions that may benefit only a single faculty member or administrative or academic department. There is an advantage to creating a separate group of faculty and staff with the right expertise to review and prioritize all technology requests based on institutional initiatives or priorities.

   Similarly, enrollment projections probably are developed by a separate group consisting of institutional research, program heads, the chief financial officer, and the chief administrative officer.

4. **Need for closure.** Peter Facione, provost at Loyola University in Chicago, offers a helpful caution about inclusion:
   While all of the foregoing approaches involve communication with many constituencies and a genuine solicitation of input, someone still has to get the budget done.

   Trustees, presidents, administrative officers, and faculty care deeply about the academic quality and long-term well-being of the institution. Students, alumni, staff, employers, and benefactors do, as well. Ultimately, however, by virtue of their expertise and the duties of their roles, major responsibility for the quality of the institution and for accomplishing its core mission rests with its faculty, administration, president, and trustees. There is a critically important difference between being a member of a constituency group that has an interest in the success of an enterprise and being one of those persons who, by virtue of the authority derived from expertise or role, are responsible for its success. Those responsible must do the work, build the budget, contribute their expertise, and take full responsibility for the results, seeking input from stakeholder groups and specialists.[3]

---

3   American Association of University Professors, "The Philosophy and Psychology of Effective Institutional Budgeting," *www.aaup.org/publications/Academe/2002/02nd/02ndfac.htm* (accessed July 5, 2006).

Roles and Responsibilities

The roles of the president and board are paramount, no matter how centralized or decentralized the budget process, as is that of the chief financial officer by virtue of responsibility and expertise. As the budgeting process becomes more participative, the roles of the campuswide budget committee and other groups on campus become more critical.

Chief executive. In a participative process, the campuswide budget committee *recommends* the budget to the chief executive. The chief executive may then decide to recommend the budget to the board (or legislature), amend it, or reject it without consulting the committee again. (Public colleges and universities usually have another intermediate level of review at the system office or state agency.) Additionally, the chief executive may impose goals or constraints. For example, the committee may be expected to develop a budget that is "balanced, invests an increasing proportion of the total budget on the academic program, limits tuition increases to consumer price inflation, and if cutbacks become necessary, maintains the existing number of faculty positions."

The president or chancellor should put these intentions in writing, discuss them with the committee at an early meeting, and communicate them more broadly in at least three ways: (1) in a charge to the committee, sometimes known as its "charter"; (2) in a letter to the campus community about the budget process (though this may be issued by the chief financial officer); and (3) through detailed budget instructions that accompany budget worksheets.

Exhibit 6.2 is a sample checklist for a president to provide to a campuswide budget committee at the start of the annual budget cycle. Note that it constitutes the "charge" to the committee.

Campuswide budget committee. The budget committee should prepare the annual budget on two levels: (1) one that encompasses tuition and salary increases, endowment use, major maintenance and capital projects, and other "macro" budget drivers; and (2) another that encompasses departmental budget recommendations about staffing levels, operating expenses, and new initiatives at the "micro" level. The relevant vice president, dean, or other senior officer should summarize and submit department requests. The committee should be limited to no more than a dozen members and should broadly represent principal campus constituencies. The president's cabinet — ordinarily consisting of vice presidents for academic affairs, admissions, advancement, finance, and student affairs — should be committee members. Additional members should be drawn from faculty, administrative and support staff, and students. Support staff (secretaries, physical plant, and dining service workers) should be represented because they often are disproportionately affected by cutbacks. If possible, members should be elected or nominated by their respective constituencies — not hand-picked or appointed. Election or nomination provides greater legitimacy and visibility for the individual and the process.

Multiyear staggered terms allow members to gain worthwhile experience. Initial elections of members can be for terms of varying lengths. For example, three faculty members may be elected for terms of one, two, and three years each.

Exhibit 6.2: Budget Committee Charge

Mission Accomplished?	YES	NO
1. **Total budget target**: Balanced by *(05-06)* _____ .	☐	☐
2. **Conceptual approach**: Start with *(04-05)* _____ estimates from last year. Adjust with premise that *(04-05)* _____ total expenses will be no more than *(03-04)* _____ budgeted expenses.	☐	☐
3. **Preliminary recommendations to the president**: Written recommendations and rationale in preliminary form by *(December 2003)* _____ . Use comparative data where possible.	☐	☐
4. **Final recommendations to the president**: *(January 2004)* _____ .	☐	☐
5. **Student fees**: Set percent increase at mid-range of markets.	☐	☐
6. **Enrollment**: Set for traditional, adult, and early college per enrollment plan.	☐	☐
7. **Endowment**: Five percent lagging 12-quarter average on *(September 30)* _____ .	☐	☐
8. **Gifts**: Set (a) $ annual giving amounts and expected percent alumni participation and (b) other gifts for current purposes.	☐	☐
9. **Employee compensation**: Set percent average compensation increase for (a) faculty and (b) staff with assumptions, if possible, for merit, cost of living, and equity portions.	☐	☐
10. **Departmental operating expense budgets**: Set average percent increase/decrease. Information Tech no lower than from *(03-04)* _____ .	☐	☐
11. **Financial aid**: (a) average grant rise no more than 25 percent over student fee rise and (b) percent change in students on financial aid equal to enrollment change.	☐	☐
12. Major maintenance: $ amount no less than *(03-04)* _____ .	☐	☐
13. **Positions**: Set # position ceilings by major division with separate ceilings for (a) faculty and (b) staff.	☐	☐
14. **Priorities**: (a) long term college viability, (b) academic programs, (c) student/life admissions, and (d) employee pay.	☐	☐
15. Debt service: Assume three-year lagging average for *04-05*	☐	☐
16. **Community Input**: At least two open meetings with community during process. Web-based "suggestion" box.	☐	☐
17. **Confidentiality**: Strict confidentiality until committee decides to communicate with community.	☐	☐
18. **Trustee involvement**: Thru CFO and chair, brief finance committee at board meetings and conference calls.	☐	☐

*Note: *Colored italics* are examples to use as a guide for checklist.

Either the chief executive or a senior faculty member should chair the committee. Having a faculty chair can help the administration gain credibility with the faculty and acknowledges the importance of the academic program in budget decisions. Presidential leadership would bestow immense status and power on the committee, but it might be difficult for the president to reject a budget submitted by a committee that he or she chaired. Although the chief financial officer should be a member of the committee — sometimes even the vice chair — contrary to conventional wisdom he or she should not be the chair. What the committee might gain in terms of expertise by this appointment, it may lose in the appearance that financial considerations will dominate.

The budget committee should spend its time deciding the budget and not arguing about the facts. The controller or budget director should be the nonvoting staff person responsible for preparing the calendar, meeting agenda, minutes, and supporting materials.

Another important staff member of the committee should be the director of institutional research or planning, who can supply much-needed comparative and historical data, a good part of which may not be financial. The budgeting process needs information on such factors as tuition-and-fee charges, staffing levels, faculty-student ratios, salary levels and increases, and budget proportions expended on instruction, research, institutional support, and other functions. Such data provide perspective and a range, both financial and political, within which the committee can make decisions.

The aim is to produce a budget that everyone supports and that surprises no one. An effective means to that end is to have committee members serving in more than one role. At Bowdoin College, the budget committee's faculty chair and student members were delegates to the board's financial planning committee. The treasurer, academic dean, and chief student affairs officer not only were members of the senior staff but also served on the budget committee and the strategic-planning task force.

Meetings of the campuswide budget committee may combine both consultative and participative approaches. These meetings may be "all campus" at a small college or "all school" at a large university. Not only should participants hear progress reports, they also should have an opportunity to speak. The committee might solicit reactions to a list (distributed in advance) of revenue and expense options under consideration, or it might post the budget on the institution's Web site and solicit opinions via a conference board or chat room on the campus intranet.

To foreclose any suspicions that the accountants are "hiding the money," the chief financial officer or a knowledgeable faculty member might offer workshops on budget practices, financial statements, and concepts relating to cost containment. In this setting, it is imperative that the budget materials be written clearly and critical terms defined. A mini-glossary should become a standard part of any handouts.

In 2001, the University of Washington posted a useful page on its Web site that addressed frequently asked questions for the community. The questions included the following:

· How big is the university's budget shortfall in the 2001 biennium?

· Why can't the state adequately fund an institution essential to Washington's economy and general welfare?

· Are funding shortfalls likely to affect the quality of education and research?

· Who will decide how resources are allocated in the coming biennium?

- Who makes the decisions about the UW's budget?

- What groups are involved in budget discussions on campus?

- Is the university considering ways of increasing revenue, aside from state appropriations?

- Is the funding shortfall likely to result in layoffs?

- Is program elimination and/or consolidation part of the university's strategy of coping with the shortfall?

- Are my benefits going to be cut?

- Am I going to get a raise this year?

- Is the state budget going to affect my retirement benefits?

- Isn't the state legislature obligated to fund the university at the levels it needs?

- How can we pay a football coach more than $1 million per year and still face cuts for the real work of the university?

- Isn't there a local rainy-day fund to cover the shortfall?

- Can we increase the number of students to increase necessary revenue?

- What departments are subject to budget cuts?[4]

Governing board. A core responsibility of the institution's governing board is to approve an annual budget. Some trustees may fear that a participative process will leave them out of the decision-making process; as a result, they may be reluctant to question a budget brought forward by a united campus. Just because the governing board officially receives the recommended budget at the end of the process, this does not mean that informal communications should not occur earlier and on several levels.

Among the questions boards should ask about the budget:

- Does the budget reflect the mission and long-term financial plan?

- Do resource-allocation decisions support the academic program?

- What long-term capital and other commitments does the budget entail? Do sufficient revenues exist to cover them?

- What contingencies exist in the budget? How does the institution propose to handle unexpected shifts in revenues or expenses during the year?

- To what extent does the budget rely on fund-raising? Does the board understand how much trustees are expected to give and influence others to give?[5]

---

[4] University of Washington, "Frequently Asked Questions," *www.washington.edu/admin/pb/budget0103/budgetfaq.htm* (accessed July 5, 2006).

[5] See: Richard T. Ingram, *Trustee Responsibilities* (Washington, D.C.: AGB, 1997).

Exhibit 6.3: Trustee Checklist on the Budget

	YES	NO
1. Budget demonstrates the college's sustainability, for example, by evidencing progress toward goals of balanced budget and 5 percent endowment allowance by FY_____.	☐	☐
2. Budget developed and framed in context of strategic plan; mission seems to fit resources and vice versa.	☐	☐
3. Budget makes successful trade-offs among student-fee increases and financial aid to increase net revenue and maintain accessibility and affordability.	☐	☐
4. Budget has realistic enrollment projections in total and for three programs; traditional, adult, and early college.	☐	☐
5. Budget has realistic assumptions about annual and capital giving.	☐	☐
6. Budget makes appropriate investments in faculty and staff compensation: (a) salaries and wages and (b) benefits.	☐	☐
7. Budget addresses deferred maintenance by appropriate investments in total key functions (for example, life safety).	☐	☐
8. Budget addresses long-term debt in terms of amount and debt service.	☐	☐
9. Budget addresses faculty and staff size and deployment with appropriate ratios (for example, student:staff) and analysis.	☐	☐
10. Budget makes good use of historical and comparative data to support key recommendations.	☐	☐
11. Budget is clear on the relationship between budget and cash flows.	☐	☐
12. Budget achieves intergenerational equity by successfully balancing short-term and long-term needs — for example, the need for affordable tuition today versus the need to lower endowment spending for tomorrow.	☐	☐
13. Budget reveals unmet needs and risks inherent in its recommendations. Honest about downsides.	☐	☐
14. Revenue and expense assumptions seem reasonable and feasible.	☐	☐
15. Overall, this budget makes me feel more knowledgeable about the finances of the university.	☐	☐

Exhibit 6.3 is a checklist that trustees and others might consider in reviewing the annual budget. It covers many of the foregoing questions, plus some subjective elements of budgetary confidence and comfort.

Board finance committee. The finance committee of the board reviews and recommends the budget to the full board. James E. Morley, Jr., the former president of the National Association of College and University Business Officers, suggests that the following encompass the responsibilities of the finance committee:

1. monitoring the institution's financial operations;

2. overseeing annual and long-range operating budgets;

3. ensuring that accurate and complete financial records are maintained;

4. ensuring that timely and accurate information is presented to the board;

5. submitting to the full board for its approval any capital budgets that have exceeded prescribed amounts; and

6. communicating with and educating the board.[6]

---

[6] James E. Morley, Jr., *The Finance Committee* (Washington, D.C.: AGB, 1997), pp. 6–8.

The finance committee's chief role is to discuss how various budget options affect not only next year's budget but the institution's long-term financial outlook as well. For example, what will be the impact in ten years of an annual spending rate of 5 percent of the endowment's market value?

The chief financial officer should consult this committee two or three times during the budgeting process about the budget's major components and campus concerns. The finance committee chair should be consulted more frequently.

Chief Financial Officer. A CFO at a college or university with a participative budget process may be in an awkward position. On the one hand, the CFO is widely perceived as the person primarily accountable for all aspects of institutional finances, including the budget. On the other hand, a participatory process disperses responsibility for budget preparation beyond the CFO to various campus constituencies, usually through a campus budget committee. The CFO must also be aware of the expectations of the chief executive and the board. How can a CFO be most effective in this situation?

· Openly support the participatory process;

· Advise the chief executive on the "charge" to the budget committee;

· Serve as the principal administrative liaison to the budget committee in terms of two-way communication about issues of process and substance;

· Ensure that new committee members are oriented to the role of the committee and fundamental financial concepts and issues;

· Provide historical, comparative, and projected budget data to the committee and campus (in cooperation with the institutional research office);

· Continually summarize the effects of committee decisions on the developing budget;

· Organize meetings for the committee to update the community and solicit feedback on tentative budget recommendations;

· Draft the recommended budget for review and endorsement by the committee before it is submitted to the chief executive and the board; and

· Lead the committee in an annual review of the process and suggestions for improvement.

Many large universities split financial responsibilities between the chief financial officer and the provost. The CFO handles the business affairs of the institution, including accounting, auditing, billing, financial reporting, and oversight of the internal office or separately incorporated foundation that manages the endowment. In part because academic affairs is the largest component of the budget, the provost as chief academic officer is responsible for budget preparation and control. In that case, the role of the CFO in a participatory budget process is assumed largely by the provost.

Other Board Committees. The budget process also should engage board committees with substantive oversight in such areas as academic affairs, student life, and buildings and grounds. The chief financial officer should update each substantive committee about the budget outlook for its area. For example, the academic affairs committee might review faculty numbers and salary pools. The chief financial officer also should update the committees about the context of the institution's total budget and other priorities to minimize "special pleading." Besides informing the budget process, involvment of board committees gives the administration multiple opportunities to convince committee members of a budget's merits before they debate and vote on the budget at the meeting of the full board.

If only the finance committee is involved in budgeting, other trustees get their first real look at the recommended budget when the board is asked to approve it. Involving them earlier at the committee level enhances their understanding and provides more opportunities for them to influence the final recommendations that go to the full board.

Balancing a budget is never easy. Beyond identifying the revenues needed to fund strategic priorities, the budget must pay for employee compensation, student services, and all the other expenses needed to operate a modern college or university. The budget must also address the competing and often conflicting concerns of a host of external and internal constituencies. It might seem too ambitious to strive to make the budget process transparent and participative under such pressure. On the contrary, an inclusive process can make a budget more realistic by taking advantage of the knowledge and experience of faculty, staff, students, and other groups. Their participation increases the likelihood that they will at least understand and support the institutional decisions the budget represents.

CHAPTER 7

Budgets in Crisis:
Coping With Financial Distress

College and universities, like corporations and other nonprofit organizations, are subject to periodic fluctuations in the economy and public support. From 2003-05, for example, higher education institutions benefited from increased alumni giving, state appropriations, endowment earnings, federal research support, and student fees.[1] This good news represented a significant upswing in funding trends. In 2000, the landscape was much grimmer: Widespread retrenchment took place as the economy worsened. Endowments eroded because of losses in the stock market, and state legislatures were confronted with huge budget shortfalls because of falling tax revenues. As Moody's Investors Services opined:

> Tuition income for many private colleges is under stress due to a
> three-year decline in household net worth, declines in employment,
> competition from public universities, and stagnant demographics in some
> parts of the country. Household net worth has declined for three years in
> a row, the first such drop since World War II.[2]

The downturn also affected public universities. In 2002, for example, Rutgers University increased tuition by 10 percent, its largest increase in a decade, in response to anemic tax revenue related to the poor economy. The institution previously had cut 75 positions in an effort to balance the budget.[3] Students and donors were forced to shoulder a larger chunk of the cost of higher education as the percentage of state budget revenues allocated to higher education declined. Thus, the question is not whether colleges and universities will confront financial problems, but rather, when and how. This chapter describes how institutions and boards can detect budgets in crisis. It provides principles for addressing the crisis through a process called "retrenchment." The chapter also outlines retrenchment stages — from minor budget shortfalls that require only a modest response to a full-blown emergency that requires significant actions to guarantee the institution's survival.

Opportunities of Retrenchment

The ultimate goal of retrenchment is to restore financial equilibrium — as evidenced by a balanced budget — achieved in conjunction with appropriate investments in salaries, maintenance, and other priorities. Raising new revenue while shrinking expenses never is easy; the task often is complicated by the necessity of maintaining community morale and public image. Still, retrenchment offers opportunities to make

---

[1] "A Year of Recovery: Special Report, Outlook 2005," *Chronicle of Higher Education* (January 7, 2005).

[2] *Moody's Higher Education Sector: 2003 Industry Outlook* (February 2003), p. 9.

[3] James M. O'Neill, "Rutgers to Increase Tuition 10 Percent," *Philadelphia Inquirer* (July 13, 2002), pp. B1-B3.

fundamental changes that would be impossible during more prosperous times. With jobs threatened, for example, faculty and staff may be more willing to reengineer or eliminate inefficient processes to save money and streamline work.

In a crisis, faculty may volunteer more eagerly to recruit students and help raise money. Trustees and regents may consider reductions in majors and programs that have high costs and low enrollment or are not central to the mission. Budgeting becomes more careful when every dollar counts, and reallocations may be eased in order to focus scarce resources on mission-critical academic programs and student services or on ventures with potential for good financial payoffs. One way to reallocate during retrenchment is to ask all departments to cut more than is needed to balance the budget and to use the excess reductions to strengthen some existing programs and invest in new ones.

Detecting Financial Distress

How can a college or university spot financial distress? The more an institution can use indicators drawn from its strategic plan, the better. Use of such indicators provides a rationale and consistency that includes standard reporting and control procedures.[4]

The prevailing measure of financial trouble is a deficit in the annual operating budget. Independent institutions label this a "decrease in operating net assets." A related measure is an increase or decrease in "total net assets," which incorporates changes in operating net assets with investment gains and losses and capital gifts. Small, sporadic deficits usually are not cause for alarm, nor is a large deficit in one year — if there are sufficient reserves or endowment to cover it. Institutions should take action when deficits (1) increase over consecutive years or (2) are greater than 5 percent to 10 percent of operating revenues.

As budgetary dependence on tuition and fees grows, a drop in student enrollment becomes significant. Bond-rating agencies deem student demand to be one of the most critical factors in assessing creditworthiness, especially in schools with high tuition dependence. Total student fees (including room and board) represent, on average, more than half of total revenue at private colleges and universities, although smaller, modestly endowed institutions often derive 80 percent or more of their revenue from this one source. Public institutions, also, are becoming more dependent on student charges as state appropriations decline. To cite a specific example, Michigan State University drew about the same proportion of its total revenue of $1.6 billion from student tuition and fees (21 percent) in 2004-05, as it did from state appropriations (23 percent).[5] In 2003-04, tuition and fees jumped 10 percent at the average four-year public institutions while state appropriations per student dropped 5 percent.[6]

---

[4] Kent John Chabotar and James P. Honan, *New Yardsticks to Measure Financial Distress.* (Washington, D.C.: American Association for Higher Education), 1996.

[5] Michigan State University, *Financial Report* (June 30, 2005), p. 15.

[6] *Trends in College Pricing* (New York: College Board, 2005), p. 24.

Tuition discounting often is highly correlated with enrollment. Institutions should carefully examine not only how many students enroll but also how much financial aid is required to recruit them. Such aid is a discount against tuition and can offset in whole or in part any revenue gained from increased enrollment. Private institutions often lose one-third or even one-half of their tuition revenue to institutional financial aid.

In sum, Moody's Investors Service suggests five warning signs of credit stress that mirror or closely parallel the warning signs of financial distress. These are (1) declining enrollment; (2) declining net tuition per student or declining net tuition revenue; (3) two consecutive years of operating deficits greater than 5 percent of revenue; (4) one year of a "serious" operating deficit, even when adding back depreciation; and (5) declining liquidity due to investment losses or operating deficits.[7]

Action: Principles of Retrenchment

Retrenchment is an organizational response to a budget crisis that aims to restore financial equilibrium — mainly through expense cuts and selected revenue increases. Every organization has specific circumstances and needs in the event of financial distress and retrenchment. Independent colleges and universities may have more flexibility to respond to a budget crisis than do public institutions, for example. On the other hand, many independent institutions have precarious finances and cannot rely on the state for survival. Still, the following principles can guide retrenchment in a wide range of organizations.[8] (These retrenchment principles will be referenced again in Chapter 8 in the case study of "McKinley College.")

1. *Retrenchment is based on hard evidence of actual or potential declines in public support, customers or clients, finances, and similar indicators.* Strategic and financial indicators flow from the strategic plan and should contain quantitative thresholds to trigger retrenchment. These might include chronic budget deficits, a downgrade in bond rating, CFI below 3, and significant enrollment shortfall. While it is foolhardy to settle on the exact response, decisions made under the duress of a financial crisis are likely to be less thoughtful and effective than those made in advance. These indicators can stand for the entire institution or any one of its units; a strong organization can have weaker parts in need of reform and retrenchment. For example, while the college as a whole might enjoy hefty budget surpluses, the bookstore and dining services may be losing money despite being designated as "profit centers."

    The catastrophic effects in 2005 of Hurricanes Katrina and Rita on Gulf Coast institutions point to a much more sudden and "natural" explanation for financial distress. In these cases, the calamities of plunging tuition revenue from departing students, losses in applicants, and the monumental

---

[7] *Moody's Higher Education Sector: 2003 Industry Outlook* (February 2003), pp. 14-15.

[8] Kent John Chabotar and James P. Honan, "Coping with Retrenchment: Strategy and Tactics," *Change* (November/December, 1990), pp. 28-34; Barbara Butterfield and Susan Wolfe, *You Can Get There from Here: The Road to Downsizing in Higher Education* (Washington, D.C.: College and University Personnel Association, 1994).

costs of reconstruction reinforce the importance of disaster preparation. Such preparations should include communications without electricity, emergency plans, business continuation insurance, redundant records and off-site storage, and legal interpretations of financial-aid commitments.[9]

2. *Mission and strategic plan significantly influence retrenchment efforts.* Any organization may be viewed as a series of concentric circles with mission-centered activities such as instruction or student services in the core circle and various extracurricular and administrative functions in the penumbra. Retrenchment protects mission-centered activities as long as possible. Retrenchment also can be an ideal opportunity to reconsider the mission: Is it too ambitious, or focused on the wrong areas?

3. *Retrenchment planning and implementation considers the possibility of future growth.* Colleges and universities are affected by such economic forces as inflation, unemployment, stock market corrections, and falling state revenues. Retrenchment decisions taken during adverse conditions should not be so drastic or permanent that the organization is impaired when conditions improve. For example, consider furloughs, job sharing, or reduced workdays as retrenchment options before terminations and layoffs, which are options the institution cannot easily reverse or change.

   Another example of temporary retrenchment is to lease out excess space, if possible, rather than selling properties. Many local school districts, for example, sold off their school buildings during the "baby bust" of the 1970s only to have to build far more expensive buildings or resort to temporary classrooms to accommodate the baby boom of the 1980s and 1990s.[10]

4. *Retrenchment is not a "quick fix."* Rather, it is a multiyear effort involving both organizational and cultural changes. Obviously, the number of years of retrenchment depends on the severity of the problem, but three to five years may not be too long — especially if the organization seeks to reengineer itself as a means of protection against future problems. Colleges and universities should fold retrenchment assumptions into the long-range plan and financial model.

   Temporarily increasing the endowment spending rate or allowing management to spend a fixed amount of quasi-endowment as a "bridge" to a more stable future can ease the pain of retrenchment. Such practices may allow the institution to reduce positions over two years rather than one, thereby maintaining services and avoiding employment panic. A one-time use of quasi-endowment to even out the effects of retrenchment, however, can become a slippery slope if it becomes a habitual means to avoid making difficult and often unpopular decisions to reduce personnel or programs.

   It is wise to consider a longer or deeper retrenchment than initially thought in order to restore a balanced budget, especially if the ameliorative actions leave the organization with no reserves, substantial deferred

[9] For more on this subject, see John Cavanaugh, "Unpredictable Is Not an Option," *Trusteeship* (November/December 2005).

[10] John H. Lindsell, *Cutback Management with an Eye to Future Growth*, doctoral thesis submitted in partial fulfillment of the requirements for the Ed.D. degree, Harvard Graduate School of Education (1990).

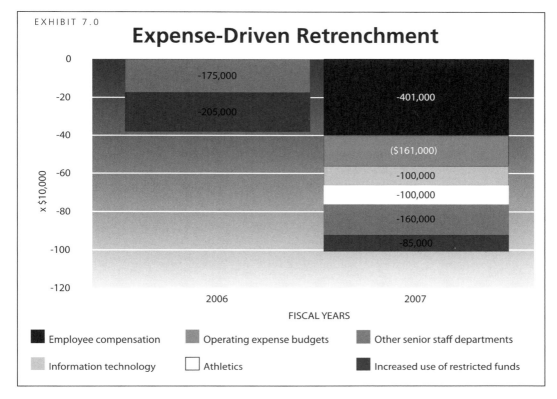

EXHIBIT 7.0

Expense-Driven Retrenchment

maintenance, or other chronic problems. The organizational focus and willingness to sacrifice will be lessened as soon as retrenchment ends and "victory" is declared.

5. *Retrenchment cuts costs before trying to increase revenues.* An institution usually can reduce its own costs more speedily and reliably than it can raise more revenue, especially from new sources. Reducing expenditures also signals to potential donors and government officials that the institution intends to become "lean and mean" before seeking new gifts or other support. This does not mean that institutions should implement all cost reductions before raising any new revenue, only that some cost reduction is addressed first. Because 50 percent or more of the budget ordinarily goes to employee compensation, cost reductions ultimately may involve position cuts and associated severance costs.

To signal that the core business will be protected, it is important to reduce administrative costs before turning to mission-centered, instructional, or student-services costs. A caveat is that it is crucial to be explicit about how such core business programs will be harmed if an administrative service on which they depend is slashed. For example, cutbacks in computing services may impair access of faculty and students to instructional technology and research databases needed for courses. Employing fewer admissions officers reduces personnel and travel costs but also risks diminishing the quality of entering students.

Exhibit 7.0 shows an expense-driven retrenchment. Forced to revise the budget to accommodate an enrollment shortfall, this college achieved

$1.4 million in budget adjustments. Most of these adjustments — and all of the initial ones — consisted of cutting expenses. Only then did the college turn to restricted funds for additional revenue.

6. *Across-the-board reductions are minimized.* When costs must be slashed without warning, an across-the-board cut is easier to accomplish than deciding what to stop doing.[11] Unfortunately, across-the-board cuts have many adverse consequences. Programs crucial to the mission are reduced by the same percentage as peripheral programs. Large programs, which are usually better able to absorb reductions, are reduced the same as smaller programs. Efficient and inefficient programs absorb the same loss. The strategic plan should determine where to take reductions in order to help institutions avoid across-the-board cutbacks that are meaningless and counterproductive.

    Faced with a budget crunch in the mid-1990s, the University of Maryland at College Park used the following criteria in deciding which academic departments to cut:

    · The centrality of each unit to the mission of the institution or to the mission of the college, school, or department in which it is located;

    · The academic strength or quality of the unit as well as the quality of its faculty as indicated by national rankings or other available measures appropriate in each program;

    · The complementary quality of the unit and the work done therein to some essential program or function performed in this institution;

    · The duplication of work done in the unit by work done elsewhere within the university system;

    · Student demand and projected enrollment in the subject matter taught in the unit;

    · Student-to-faculty ratio in the unit;

    · Comparative cost analysis/effectiveness of the unit; and

    · Any potential impact on equity that the proposed number of terminations would have on a unit, department, or college.[12]

7. *"Growth by substitution:" Some programs develop or expand at the expense of others.* An internally generated source of revenue that can forestall some cutbacks during the retrenchment process is termed growth by substitution. Under this strategy, programs and services viewed as central to the institution's strategic priorities

---

[11] Robert Dickeson, *Prioritizing Academic Programs and Services*, presentation at AGB's Annual Workshop for Board Members and Institutional Leaders of Independent Colleges and Universities (November 10, 2003). See also Robert Dickeson, *Prioritizing Academic Programs and Services* (San Francisco: Jossey-Bass, 1999), p. 44.

[12] University of Maryland at College Park, *Consolidated USMH & UMCP Policies and Procedures Manual*, "Procedures for the Termination of Faculty Appointments during Fiscal Crisis" (February 1995).

are preserved or even expanded — by cutting elsewhere. On the academic side, for example, this may mean dropping one or two underenrolled departments to support other academic programs and support services.

8. *Retrenchment recognizes that more revenues often mean higher costs.* How much will it cost to launch that new annual giving program or capital campaign to fund the strategic plan? What will be the net cost savings from position cuts after deducting severance and replacement costs? The term "net" is essential in a financial manager's lexicon. While more commonly applied to the residual value of buildings (after depreciation and discounts), net also applies to revenues and cost savings.

9. *Quality issues are as important as the issues of revenues or costs.* What is quality in higher education? The best measures reside in the institution's own list of strategic indicators. Other indicators of quality are accreditation (both institutional and departmental), academic reputation as measured by the annual *U.S. News & World Report* rankings, student retention and graduation rates, and the number of grants and prizes awarded to faculty. In deciding where to cut expenses, colleges and universities must seek to minimize harm to whatever they define as high quality. For example, though cutting staff in the controller's or human resources office will adversely affect the finance and personnel functions to some extent, such cuts probably are less damaging than reductions in faculty or instructional technology positions.

10. *People and groups potentially affected by retrenchment should participate in key decisions.* Broad participation is as needed in retrenchment as it is in budgeting. Although staff may be protective of their departments, they cannot complain they were not asked for input. Remarkably good advice about potential revenues and cost savings often results from staff participation. Support staff should be especially encouraged to participate because they often know programs and services better than management and thus can more readily identify redundancies and inefficiencies. A study of institutional handbooks, union contracts, and meeting laws is crucial before deciding on the level of participation.

11. *The board and administration should actively support the retrenchment effort.* Retrenchment cannot succeed without the visible backing of top management and the board. The chief executive — not the chief financial officer — should announce decisions about the retrenchment in open meetings and campus media. The board should endorse the reductions as part of the annual budget process or review of the long-range plan. The logic of the cuts and the best intentions of the organization may speak for themselves, but board leadership commands the respect and power to ensure that retrenchment decisions will be executed promptly.

12. *Retrenchment decisions are disseminated immediately using a variety of media and methods.* Consistent with organizational policies and contracts, significant reductions should be announced as soon as possible after the decision to make them.

These include immediate cuts in staff positions or budgets as well as tentative decisions on long-term reductions. Otherwise, rumors will circulate that the cuts are deeper or in areas different than actually is the case. The president and the board must also be certain that the cuts are essential, be conscious of staff morale and public perceptions, and prepared to explain the actions in the most positive light that is reasonable under the circumstances. Here are two examples of what not to do:

- Under an inexperienced president, one college laid off half its construction and maintenance staff without warning or consultation, only to have to restore most of the positions within six months when workloads became unwieldy.

- Another college reduced 100 positions by having supervisors bring the affected staff to a central location so they could be told they were being terminated. Neither the supervisors nor the staff members had any idea that this drastic action was even contemplated. This was cited as one reason behind the president's resignation after less than two years in office.

Many of the principles of retrenchment — attention to mission, basing decisions on data, and including stakeholders — apply to growth, too. Just because enrollment is booming or fund-raising has soared does not automatically mean that new programs unrelated to the mission should be started.

Phases of Retrenchment

A helpful framework for deciding where to retrench is one that unfolds in discrete phases, beginning with relatively easy, painless changes and proceeding gradually to the most serious revenue and expense actions that may threaten the institution's long-term sustainability.

None of these phases or actions is fixed, of course, and institutions often alter the list or the order to fit their circumstances, culture, and history. Colleges and universities are well served when they link different phases to strategic indicators. For example, a $100,000 budget shortfall might trigger a Phase 1 response, whereas a $1 million shortfall would prompt quick adoption of Phase 1 and Phase 2 responses.

Phase 1: Slowdown. This first phase, usually perceived as a short-term phenomenon, occurs when the need to retrench first becomes apparent. An example might be that of a small, private college coping with an enrollment shortfall of 25 students. One possible action is to raise targets for net income from auxiliary enterprises such as the bookstore, summer programs, and annual giving. Another small retrenchment step might be to use contingency funds that were established for this very purpose. Purchases and new hires also may be deferred.

Phase 2: Yellow Alert. In this phase, the need for retrenchment continues or is more serious. A large budget deficit, loss of endowment market value, or a second consecutive enrollment shortfall are examples of events that might set off a Phase 2 response. Concerns over bond ratings and outlooks also might kick in at this point.

While bond ratings may be preserved, the rating agency may downgrade the outlook from stable to negative.

Again, goals for auxiliary programs and annual giving might be raised. The institution may ask the state for advance funding of annual appropriations or for other support. Student fees might be increased or new fees imposed. The board might authorize a one-time use of quasi-endowment or an increase in endowment spending to rebuild a bridge to financial equilibrium. Alternatively, the institution may utilize contingency funds. To meet payroll and balance the operating budget, the board may need to redouble its efforts to the extent of mounting a kind of "treasure hunt" to find available funds from plant reserves that were set aside in previous years for major maintenance and capital projects, other restricted funds, or endowments.

On the expense side, debt refinancing might save significant amounts if interest rates are favorable. Deferrals might be extended to maintenance projects and even replacement hires. Projected increases in salaries and wages may be postponed, and annual and temporary positions may be eliminated. The institution also may choose to offer an early retirement package — presumably with the aim of payback in three years or so — after accounting for salary savings and severance costs.

Outsourcing and partnering arrangements are also tactics that may reduce costs, reallocate resources, and improve quality.[13] Nowadays, most colleges and universities outsource at least some nonacademic services.

Phase 3: Red Alert. Retrenchment is prolonged and severe at this phase. Enrollment shortfalls persist or have worsened, and financial-aid costs skyrocket because the institution must "buy" a first-year class. The effects are serious: The bond rating is downgraded and the budget remains unbalanced for consecutive years — or balanced only by deferring maintenance, overspending from the endowment, or freezing salaries and benefits.

In this phase, retrenchment actions from the first and second phases continue and expand. The institution's mission may show noticeable damage, having been narrowed considerably or ignored altogether. Endowment spending may reach unsustainable levels of 10 percent or greater, and short-term borrowing increases. Land and buildings may be sold, salary increases eliminated, and across-the-board cuts proposed. Reductions affect regular positions — starting with administrative positions — with the understanding that these cuts may affect services. Academic programs may be cut, with interdisciplinary departments more vulnerable than entrenched, discipline-based departments.

Evergreen State College in Washington has a step-by-step procedure if state allocation falls "to such low levels that it seems that reducing the size of the faculty may be financially unavoidable."[14] Before the trustees formally consider such a decision, faculty are contacted to determine if they are willing to retire early, teach

---

[13] Thomas A. McLaughlin, *Nonprofit Mergers and Alliances: A Strategic Planning Guide* (New York: Wiley, 1996); and Mary F. Bushman and John E. Dean, "Outsourcing of Non-Mission Critical Functions" in *Course Corrections: Experts Offer Solutions to the College Cost Crisis* (Indianapolis: Lumina Foundation for Education, 2005).

[14] Evergreen State College, "Faculty Reduction in Force Policy," adopted by the faculty in May 1995. *Faculty Handbook*, 2006. *www.evergreen.edu/policies/f-3400.htm* (accessed July 6, 2006.)

part-time for some period in a way that meets the curricular needs of the college, or go on voluntary leave without pay. The college uses such voluntary adjustments to alleviate the budget crisis before declaring financial exigency and resorting to involuntary personnel reductions. If the crisis persists, the college then proceeds to make reductions in this order:

1. Termination of adjunct, visiting, and post-retirement faculty contracts.

2. Elimination of regular faculty on term appointments.

3. Involuntary furloughs for regular faculty on continuing appointments.

4. Reorganization of the college: If the preceding steps are not sufficient to produce the necessary budget cuts, the faculty — in consultation with students and staff — prepare a new long-term curriculum plan. This reorganizes the curriculum and other aspects of the academic program so that the college can function with drastically reduced funding levels.[15]

Phase 4: Emergency. Actions taken in earlier phases become more acute: Admissions become essentially open, and tuition discounting accelerates. Position reductions result in elimination of services and departments or in expanded outsourcing. Temptation grows stronger to use endowment principal, tap unexpended grant funds, and assume greater debt in order to raise cash for operations.

Some colleges that found themselves in Phase 4, however, have retrenched successfully. Champlain College in Vermont, for example, turned chronic budget deficits into surpluses by eliminating tenure, varsity sports, and a dozen marginal majors to maintain relatively low tuition.[16] This was strategic because the college sought to gain a competitive advantage and increase net revenue by offsetting the price reduction with increased enrollment and lower financial-aid costs.

If closure is not imminent, an institution also may explore mergers with other institutions. In recent years, for example, Mount Vernon College was acquired by George Washington University, Marymount College by Fordham University, and the College of Insurance by St. John's University.[17]

A Sample Scoring System. Most colleges and universities will want to take a flexible approach to deciding which phase is most relevant to their situation. In some cases, a catastrophic collapse of a single indicator (enrollment is a good example) might lead to a Phase 4 response, while in other cases this same collapse could be ameliorated by a large endowment gift or state aid. Exhibit 7.1 shows how an institution might make sense of widespread variations in strategic indicators.

Identification of prime strategic indicators and a sense of how much deterioration it would take to declare a specific indicator no longer to be in a "slow down" phase but in "emergency" status is the essence of the spreadsheet. The strategic

---

[15] *Ibid.*

[16] Symonds, *op. cit.*, p. 75.

[17] Moody's Investors Service, *Higher Education Sector: 2003 Industry Outlook* (February 2003), p. 14.

Exhibit 7.1 Sample Retrenchment Scoring

Strategic Indicator	Speed Up	Points	Slow Down	Points	Yellow Alert	Points	Red Alert	Points	Emergency	Points
Change In Net Operating Assets	5%	10	-2%	-4	-4%	-8	-10%	-20	-15%	-30
Change In Total Net Assets	5%	8	-3%	-5	-4%	-6	-6%	-10	-10%	-16
Net Tuition Per Student	3%	7	-1%	-2	-2%	-5	-3%	-7	-5%	-12
Enrollment	5%	10	-2%	-4	-4%	-8	-6%	-12	-10%	-20
Acceptance Rate	-2%	2	0%	1	2%	-2	5%	-4	8%	-6
Yield Rate	2%	2	-2%	-2	-3%	-3	-5%	-5	-8%	-8
Endowment Per Student	5%	5	0%	-1	-5%	-5	7%	7	-10%	-10
Facility Condition Index (FCI)	-2%	4	2%	-4	3%	-6	4%	-8	5%	-10
Alumni Giving Rate	1%	2	-1%	-2	-2%	-4	-3%	-6	-4%	-8
Threshold:				-15		-35		-50		-85

indicators and percentages, however, are only illustrative. An important feature is the first column of "speed up," which assumes that, except for a financial "meltdown," some indicators may still move in a positive direction.

A second feature is the use of "points" for each strategic indicator at each phase. This accounts for the large disparities likely in performance and the need for a rough "threshold" for declaring the institution to be in a certain phase and to take the actions discussed earlier in the chapter. Thus, the accumulation of minus 15 points in this approach is the threshold for "slow down." This allows deteriorations at varying rates to be assigned different priorities. For example, a 4 percent downturn in operating net assets ("yellow alert") is minus 8 points, but a 10 percent drop in total net assets is minus 16 points ("emergency"). Finally, positive results in the "speed up" column can partly offset the negative results elsewhere — for example, a 5 percent gain in endowment per student yields 5 points.

The budget retrenchment needed to restore financial equilibrium presents opportunities to shift priorities and change program arrays. Still, no college or university wants to endure financial distress — no matter how predictable — given normal economic ebbs and flows. The process can be traumatic in financial and human terms, especially when it leads to reductions in faculty and staff. The retrenchment process can be effective to the extent that the institution has defined clear measures for detecting financial distress and knows how it will respond depending on the severity of the circumstances. Most crucially, boards and presidents must base actions on reliable data and analysis of the probable effects of retrenchment on institutional mission and strategy.

CHAPTER 8

The Strategy-Focused Organization: A Case Study

Failure to think strategically about financial issues is especially troublesome as colleges and universities confront a fluctuating economy, uncertain government support, variable student and parent expectations, and similar concerns. While strategic planning and budgeting does not remove financial uncertainties, it does allow the institution to focus its strengths and attention on dealing with them most effectively.

This chapter begins with a hypothetical case of a postsecondary institution — McKinley College — that is facing crises in leadership, governance, and finance. Learning points from four areas covered in the previous chapters are summarized in terms of how they apply to the case of McKinley College: financial analysis, strategic planning, strategic budgeting, and retrenchment.[1]

Case Study: McKinley College

Background. Founded in 1857, McKinley College is an independent college of 2,500 undergraduate students with an annual budget of $55 million. There are two undergraduate student populations: traditional students 18 to 22 years-old and adults older than 23.

After a decade of little or no growth, the traditional student numbers have skyrocketed with an enrolled first-year class of 440 — compared with 325 budgeted and 290 enrolled the previous year. Applications have jumped to 2,400 in each of the last two years, from a typical 1,200 to 1,400. About two-thirds of the students are from out of state, though 50 percent of all students are from three states — the college's home state and the two adjacent states to the north and south. The admission rate is 70 percent, but only 27 percent of those admitted actually enrolled last year. In terms of average high school grades and the percentage of students in the top 10 percent of their class, quality has improved.

The adult education program has boomed in the last five years, growing from 250 students to 1,200. Adult students take an average of 10.6 credits per semester when 12 credits is considered full-time. Their tuition is less than a third of that charged to traditional students, but after counting financial aid that is directed largely to traditional students, the actual price paid per credit hour is relatively similar. The adults also have a higher college grade-point average and, adjusted for their part-time status, have higher five-year and six-year graduation rates than traditional students. The adult program is very diverse, with about 75 percent women and 40 percent students of color.

---

[1] Commentary is based in part on the discussions that involved hundreds of trustees and presidents who encountered a version of McKinley College case at AGB's "Seminar for New Trustees," at the 2006 National Conference on Trusteeship.

U.S. News & World Report considers McKinley College to be a Tier 3 institution among national liberal arts colleges with a rank ranging between 120 and 130. Although lacking a formal strategic plan, the college successfully concluded a $50 million capital campaign two years ago. The endowment is $50 million with a 5 percent spending rate (based on a lagging three-year average) that has been cut from 14 percent in four years. About 75 percent of the college's revenue comes from student fees, with the rest from annual giving, endowment earnings, and other sources. (This budget does not include research grants or self-funded auxiliaries.) McKinley College has a 23-college comparison group (14 peer and 9 aspirant colleges), while its fees are slightly above, and its endowment value slightly below, the group's average.

There are 400 faculty and staff (two-thirds of the faculty are tenured), and the student-to-teacher ratio is 15 to 1. Employee salaries and benefits account for about two-thirds of the budget but, except for assistant professors and support staff, badly trail their respective markets. The college's debt burden is high at $30 million; it has a minimum investment-grade bond rating of BBB.

McKinley College has not been able to control its capital projects. The previous administration had planned a classroom building that was initially budgeted at $6 million, but after construction began, this figure was revised upward to $9 million. Final cost of the project came to around $13 million, most of which the college had to borrow. Deferred maintenance is about $2 million on a physical plant with a replacement value of $100 million.

The college faces a $2 million deficit for the upcoming fiscal year. An economic downturn threatens the college's financial equilibrium in several areas:

- Financial aid is skyrocketing. Institutional grant aid effectively discounts tuition by 45 percent, thus lowering net tuition. The state provides a $3,000 legislative grant to every resident who attends McKinley, which partly offsets the discount.

- College costs are a major financial and political issue. Like most colleges, McKinley has increased student fees 4 percent to 6 percent per year for decades, at least for traditional students. Because McKinley is not among the most selective colleges, financial aid increasingly has been used to attract good students. It also has helped to promote a diverse student body. With the annual "sticker price" for student fees near $30,000 (including room and board), many worry how much longer McKinley can continue to hike fees at the same rate.

- Another challenge is heightened competition from the lower cost, excellent public universities in the state. A decade ago, only the flagship state university was among the top ten "overlap" colleges to which traditional applicants to McKinley also applied. Today, seven of the ten overlap colleges are state institutions. Although the burgeoning adult program generally is perceived as superior to the local competition, both public and private, the dean for continuing education wonders whether McKinley can retain its current market share.

- A different aspect of McKinley's costs is the curriculum. Ranging from business and natural sciences to humanities, social sciences, and the arts, the curriculum contains 80 majors and other programs. Faculty explain that they added the programs at the behest of the admissions office to attract students, while the administration complains that the faculty seem unwilling to reduce the number even when enrollment is booming. Eighty programs are far above the number at comparable schools; the menu of offerings is large relative to the number of faculty.

· The endowment is worth 10 percent less than it was this time last year, thus cutting the income available for the budget even with a lagging-average spending formula.

· Utility and healthcare costs are running 20 percent higher than expected. The costs of employee and retiree health insurance have soared.

· Hiring authority is decentralized, with the central finance office not approving position postings. This has led to 20 unbudgeted positions, almost all administrative staff.

Budgeting Process. The annual budget is prepared by the chief financial officer starting in December and is discussed extensively with the president and academic dean. (A small budget committee of faculty and mid-level administrators is used occasionally to advise on specific issues, such as tuition and fee and salary increases). The chief financial officer recommends the budget for the next fiscal year to the board of trustees in February after a review and approval by the finance committee.

Recommended Budget. President Elizabeth Hanna has been in office for five years and expects the economic downturn to persist for the next three years and probably beyond. At the February meeting of the board, the chief financial officer presents the annual budget that contains what he terms a "$2 million solution" to the crisis. On the revenue side, the proposal includes (1) gradual enrollment growth to 3,000 undergraduates with the same proportions of traditional and adult students, (2) increases of 0.5 percent in student fees to 4.5 percent and endowment spending to 5.5 percent, and (3) intensified fund-raising. Expense reductions involved (1) one-time deferrals of equipment purchases and maintenance projects; (2) layoff of ten faculty and staff plus a hiring freeze; (3) a 2 percent across-the-board cut in administrative departments, although not in the academic program; and (4) elimination of varsity sports in wrestling, gymnastics, and tennis.

Trustee Reaction. Heated discussions ensue about the merits of the recommended budget. The chair of the academic affairs committee insists that retrenchment should protect academic program and faculty positions, as they constitute the core business of the college. An ally of the chair of the faculty senate, the committee chair asserts that the continuing-education program is "open admissions" and lacks standards. After defending student programming and residential life as part of the core business, the student affairs committee chair says he believes that the 80 majors and concentrations in the academic program are too elaborate for the college.

The chair of the admissions and financial-aid committee rejects major expense reductions as impairing program quality and student applications. Although financial aid is not among the cuts, she fears that a less attractive academic and student affairs program will mean more preferential packaging of financial aid to maintain enrollment. The development committee chair worries about balancing the budget through increased fund-raising in tough economic times. The finance committee chair argues against trying to balance the budget in a single year; he supports the proposal to increase enrollment but questions keeping the existing proportions of traditional and adult students. Both the president and the board chair are dismayed by the lack of consensus.

Imagine that you are a consultant to the board. The executive committee asks for your advice with the understanding that you are not limited to the options discussed at the meeting. They provide you with the financial indicators in Exhibit 8.0 with five-year projections assuming that present trends continue.

Study Questions

1. *Financial Analysis.* Analyze McKinley College's financial indicators. What are the greatest strengths and weaknesses, currently and in five years?

2. *Strategic Planning.* What do you think about the condition of McKinley officials' strategic thinking and their ability to address internal or environmental issues? What does your financial analysis suggest about the need for strategic planning?

3. *Strategic Budgeting.* How strategic is the budget process? Comment on the strengths and weaknesses of the budget process. How can McKinley restore the budget to financial equilibrium?

4. *Retrenchment.* To what extent do the chief financial officer's recommendations and the resulting trustee debate reflect the principles of retrenchment?

Financial Analysis: Summary

Strategic indicators are derived directly from the plan, but not all financial indicators are strategic. Effective planning defines strategic indicators for the institution and a comparison group with which to compare performance. These achievements can be end-result outcomes or, more likely, indicators that show the budget's relevance to intermediate financial and program goals and key stakeholders inside and outside the institution. Financial indicators can exist without a plan (as is the situation at McKinley College) but still measure the budget, debt, enrollment, and other key data.

The CASH acronym suggests the four ways an institution can evaluate its strategic and financial indicators: comparatively with similar institutions, with reference to a national average or industry standard, and historically within the same institution over time. Financial assumptions embedded in the plan can be double-checked by going back three to five years and pretending that you do not know the actual revenues and expenses today. Which forecasting assumption would have most accurately predicted net tuition revenue, appropriations, annual giving, and other budget items?

Financial Analysis at McKinley College: Commentary

McKinley confronts a financial crisis. This is reflected most starkly in the projected declines in net assets, bond rating, facilities condition, and endowment per student. Contributing factors are an endowment growth slower than the growth in debt, enrollment, or the budget, significant faculty hiring that lowers the student-to-faculty ratio, and a burgeoning tuition-discount rate.

From a balanced operating budget this year (0 percent), the college expects a decline in operating net assets of 15 percent in five years. This contributes to a diminution in total net assets of 10 percent by the same year. Remember that total net assets add endowment gains or losses and new capital gifts to operating net assets.

Debt is expected to rise to $35 million in five years, but there is no mention of the purpose. If incurred for revenue-producing activities such as student residence halls, the higher debt burden would not be as troubling.

The rise in debt coupled with drops in net assets is contributing to an anticipated downgrade of bond rating to BBB-, a rating that falls below investment grade. This downgrade will drive up interest costs and contribute to the losses in net assets because many institutional investors will not buy bonds below investment grade.

The tuition discount jumps from 45 percent to 50 percent in five years, thereby adding $2 million in expenses that about equals next year's projected deficit of $2 million.

The facilities condition index (FCI) rises from 2 percent to greater than 4 percent in five years. It divides the replacement value of the buildings (in this year, $100 million) by the amount of deferred maintenance ($2 million this year). While any rating below 5 percent is considered "good," doubling the FCI is a concern and may be a harbinger of a deteriorating physical plant. That the budget is so unbalanced even with this deferral of investments in maintenance adds to the appearance of crisis.

Endowment per student is among the most powerful signs of institutional financial strength. At McKinley, it is projected to fall from $23,000 this year to less than $21,800 in five years. (See Exhibit 8.0.) Assuming annual inflation, the drop is even worse in "constant" dollars. The rise in endowment market value to $58 million in five years (16 percent) trails increases in enrollment (20 percent) and the annual budget (19 percent). A comparison of endowment per student with peers and competitors reveals that McKinley is lagging badly.

A positive sign is that tuition and fees (including room and board) seem competitive with peers and aspirants. In fact, there seems to be some room to increase fees even more rapidly and still be below the averages of both sets of competitors.

Another positive indicator is the projected improvement in the student-to-faculty ratio to 12 to 1, although the amount of faculty hiring needed to accomplish this ratio is obviously contributing to the financial crisis.

Other positive indicators are projected increases in the percentage of alumni contributing to 25 percent and total gifts to $5 million. The current alumni giving rate of 21 percent is below that of last year as well as below the averages of peer and

Exhibit 8.0: Financial Indicators at McKinley College

Internal Indicator	In Five Years	This Year	Last Year
1. Enrollment	3,000	2,500	2,250
2. Annual budget	$65mm	$55mm	$52mm
3. Level of debt	$35mm	$30mm	$29.0M
4. Bond rating	BBB-	BBB	BBB
5. Tuition discount	50%	45%	45%
6. Facilities Condition Index	4.5%	2%	1%
7. Change in operating net assets/revenue	-15%	0%	3%
8. Change in total net assets/revenue	-10%	5%	-2%

Comparative Indicator	In Five Years	This Year	Last Year	Peer Avg. This Year — Range	Peer Avg. This Year — Rank (of 14)	Aspirant Avg. This Year — Range	Aspirant Avg. This Year — Rank (of 9)
9. Tuition and fees	$24,260*	$21,640	$20,270	$22,703		$26,941	
				$14,669-$32,724	10	$16,684-$32,659	8
10. Room and board	$7,700*	$6,530	$6,330	$7,146		$8,360	
				$5,430-$11,986	10	$6,426-$11,464	8
11. E&G revenues*/student FTE *net of financial aid	$14,900	$12,595	$12,099	$14,700		$20,241	
				$10.0-$20.1	13	$15.1-$26.7	9
12. Amount of endowment	$58.0mm	$50.0mm	$54.9mm	$11.4		$136M	
				$22.0-$651.0M	9	$59.9-$258M	8
13. *Endowment per student FTE*	$21,800*	$23,000	$26,400	$79,301		$58,641	
				$16,174-$123,925	8	$27.5-$87.4	8
14. *% of alumni making contributions*	25%	21%	24%	26%		30%	
				15%-35%	8	13%-49%	8
15. Total gifts	$5mm	$3.5mm	$3mm	$5.6M		$8.7M	
				$3.0-$11.6M	3	$3.0-$17.4M	5
16. *Average faculty salary* (all ranks combined)	$63,700	$48,849	$45,000	$56,767		$62,767	
				$44.2-$65.7	11	$58.8-$72.7	8
17. *Student/faculty ratio*	12/1	15/1	14/1	15.0/1		10.3/1	
				13/1-25.2/1	11	13/1-25.2/1	11

Italics = indicator counts are used in the *U.S. News & World Report* rankings.

aspirant colleges. Gift amounts also are below the competition. However, as with the other indicators, the deteriorating overall financial condition may well have a negative effect if alumni and other donors lose confidence.

Strategic Planning: Summary

Strategic planning helps the institution manage change in response to environmental conditions and internal pressures for quality, efficiency, and other priorities. It identifies how the college or university differs from the competition. It harnesses vision and data to make fundamental choices about students and programs that can transform the institution. Many planning processes fail because they have too many goals or unrealistic ones, lack access to top decision makers, and overlook political and financial constraints.

A strategic plan contains a mission, goals and objectives, and the programs and policies needed to attain them, and it names who is responsible for the execution of the plan. It proceeds from prior plans and current needs in tandem with an honest assessment of environmental allies, adversaries, and the market in which the college or university competes. By linking money with mission, the financial plan "costs" the strategic plan, and in so doing becomes a major determinant of its feasibility. Financial planning requires decisions on the major budget drivers, assumptions about rates of increase or decrease, the forecast time period (which is often the same as that for the strategic plan), and the accuracy and comparability of the data used to drive the analysis.

Strategic Planning at McKinley College: Commentary

The lack of a strategic plan at McKinley makes the chief financial officer's budget proposals ad hoc and reactive. The institution cannot place its response to the fiscal crisis in terms of how any action, or inaction, will affect mission and goals. There is no basis on which to fix priorities.

What are McKinley's mission and core values? They must speak to the college's uniqueness and basis for attracting new students and financial support. The institution must avoid the temptation to reflect only the status quo in the mission but rather should focus on areas of actual or potential strength. Two areas worth considering are the inclusion of both business and art in the curriculum ("practical liberal arts") and the benefits of having traditional and adult students in the same classes ("lifelong education").

The plan must contend with a host of strategic issues. The breadth of curriculum, types of students, pricing, tuition discounting, enrollment growth, and competition (especially with the state's public institutions) are important issues for the plan to address.

The relationship of the traditional and adult programs and their respective quality and outcomes must be studied. Even though the traditional program has experienced recent growth, much of the institution's financial equilibrium has been achieved by the surge in adult enrollment. And though the adult students are excelling academically, the change is threatening and needs to be better planned and explained. The benefits of a mixed-age population in terms of learning and career development must be part of the message.

Whether the college grows to 3,000 depends on whether one or both programs have the potential to become larger and still preserve quality. Can McKinley aspire to rise higher than Tier 3 in *U.S. News*? Which majors and other programs have the highest enrollment potential? How can tuition discounting be controlled?

Despite the availability of the financial data, much of the discussion seems not to be based on actual data. There are numerous assertions offered with anecdotal evidence or opinions rather than survey or other data. Any sense of student or institutional outcomes seems lost in the shuffle. An office of institutional research, drawing on institutional and comparative data, should prepare a "fact book" and other materials for the board so that data — not myth — influence decision making. The auditors might be asked to confirm current and historical revenues and expenses, as well as the market value of the endowment and replacement value of the physical plant to aid the analysis.

Can the institution afford to wait the one or two years that planning will take before the task of addressing the fiscal crisis becomes another critical issue for the college? President Hanna might consider forming task forces of trustees and campus groups to address short-term problems that will balance the budget and the long-term issues that must be tackled in the strategic plan. A larger group, if not the full board, would integrate the results of these efforts and define mission and core values that emerge in the process. Alternatively, the mission and values might be identified before the task forces are formed to serve as guideposts for their individual efforts.

The resulting plan should have no more than 15 strategic indicators to cover admissions, advancement, finance, student services, and the academic program. Among the most prevalent are admissions and yield rates, average SAT and secondary school grades of the entering class, student-to-faculty ratio and average class size, percentage increases in net operating and total net assets, endowment per student, and percentage of active alumni who contribute. Any overlap between the strategic indicators and, for example, ratios needed for a higher bond rating — BBB is minimum investment grade — or higher *U.S. News* ranking should be noted.

Strategic Budgeting: Summary

The achievement of financial equilibrium is budgeting's prime goal. This concept starts with a balanced budget that still makes appropriate investments in salaries and wages, maintenance, and other core priorities. True equilibrium should not be achieved through excessive hikes in student fees or overwrought spending from the endowment or foundation base.

The essence of strategic budgeting is its explicit link to the institution's strategic plan. A strategic budget consistently refers to the mission and values as well as the long-range financial plan to justify expected revenues and expenses. It synchronizes budgeted revenues and expenses with board investment policies and the long-term outlook for the endowment and shows the assumptions and risks underlying budget recommendations. It distinguishes between continuing and one-time revenues and expenses, and it provides for contingency funds and reserves by not budgeting vacancy savings, assuming lower-than-expected enrollment, and basing utility budgets on extreme weather conditions. An effective strategic budget explains the comparative data and benchmarks used.

How a budget is assembled or created is also of great consequence. A campus community is more likely to understand and accept a budget it has helped develop, and such a budget may more accurately reflect campus realities, thus clarifying the rationale for budget priorities. A budgeting process also can be educational by introducing everyone to the terms and concepts of financial management. In the most participative approach, faculty and staff draft the budget, typically by forming a committee and holding hearings, and recommend the budget to the chief executive and trustees.

Strategic Budgeting at McKinley College: Commentary

McKinley has problems and opportunities in almost every aspect of financial planning and budgeting. The development of a strategic plan will help enormously, but more immediate steps also seem necessary.

Financial equilibrium must be restored. McKinley must fix projected decreases in operating and net assets. The decreases are contributing to the drop in the bond rating and may have cascading effects on bond interest costs, rise in endowment market value, alumni and donor confidence, endowment per student, and other crucial variables.

McKinley should be commended for striving not only for a balanced budget but also for true financial equilibrium by making investments in salaries and maintenance and by not balancing the budget "on the backs" of students by excessive tuition increases or on the endowment by unwarranted spending way beyond 5 percent.

Strategic budgeting can be promoted even in the absence of a plan if the president and board achieve consensus on a short-term direction and priorities. The college can then make budget decisions in a strategic context. For example, McKinley may decide to concentrate on its preprofessional programs as a market niche, increase enrollment, reduce tuition discounting, and recruit faculty.

As it moves forward, any retrenchment program should begin with expense reductions. Any reduction in the number of academic programs below 80 will promote focus but not save much in compensation because faculty hiring is destined to grow with enrollment. The academic fields the new faculty represent may change, however. A careful market analysis of the breadth of curricular offerings at top competitor institutions will help to decide the number and kinds of academic programs McKinley College offers.

Criteria for program prioritization that leads to reductions, additions, and changes in the budget should be developed and approved before data are applied. This strategy lessens the opportunity to reject the criteria because of anticipated effects on particular programs (majors and concentrations) and interests. Among the criteria to be considered for each program are external demand, quality of program outcomes such as graduation rates and performance on standardized tests, revenue and costs, and analysis of the opportunities created by the environment on which the institution might capitalize.[2]

The 50 percent tuition-discount rate obviously is unacceptable. Even the current 45 percent discount is above the national average and will complicate balancing the budget until it is reduced. A gradual reduction of one to two percentage points per year up to 40 percent is possible and would save $2 million or more per year. The surge in applications seems to support a cut. It will be essential for McKinley to model the probable effects of alternative financial-aid packages. On what types of students, for example, should admissions focus its financial-aid dollars? What combinations of merit and need-based grant aid will best attract good students? How can McKinley use merit aid to attract high-income and low-need students? What are the strategic consequences?

The enrollment-growth scenario should be reexamined, given the deterioration in operating net assets as well as endowment per student. Perhaps the need to "buy" these students with excessive tuition discounting suggests another approach to student recruitment that takes advantage of "practical liberal arts" and other unique features of McKinley. In addition, an analysis of the net contribution of the traditional and adult programs might suggest proportionally more growth in adult students, a prime source of diversity as well. On the other hand, such an analysis also might suggest total enrollment above 3,000, which might increase net revenue if the college addresses the foregoing concerns.

In five years, the physical plant will still be in "good" condition, as least as revealed by an FCI of 4.5 percent. In fact, some selective deferrals in maintenance expenses over a limited time may help relieve the immediate financial pressure. If we assume that the replacement value of the plant, after deducting depreciation and adding new facilities and renovations, remains at $100 million in five years, McKinley could add $5 million in deferred maintenance and not even drop below a "fair" rating (between 5 percent and 10 percent of replacement value). While not the wisest course over the long term, modestly increasing deferred maintenance could produce funds to help balance the budget and "buy time" for the president and board to engage in strategic planning.

Although cutting the student-to-faculty ratio to 12 to 1 will improve instruction and probably support enrollment growth and student retention, this is unaffordable. Maintaining this year's ratio of 15 to 1 will save millions and still leave McKinley's ratio at the average of peer institutions, though the ratio is much worse than that of aspirant colleges and universities. A 15 to 1 ratio also will make it easier to reach faculty salary targets so that the faculty are better compensated and more easily retained.

Other ways to restore financial equilibrium in the near term include examining the asset allocation of the endowment to determine if returns meet industry standards

---

[2] Robert C. Dickeson, *Prioritizing Academic Programs and Services* (San Francisco: Jossey-Bass, 1999), pp. 59–75.

consistent with acceptable risk, working to improve alumni giving beyond 25 percent (that may be aided by a new strategic plan), and intensifying gift solicitation. New revenues from annual and capital giving should precede any move to hike endowment spending much above 5 percent even temporarily.

Capacity may exist to increase student fees more rapidly than 4 percent, given current higher average fees for traditional students among peers and aspirants. Even a 1 percent rise to 5 percent would add about $250,000 in annual revenue even after the tuition discount. Often, the finance staff will argue for higher fee increases (in order not to "leave money on the table"), while admissions staff want to keep the rise as low as possible to boost the number of applicants. Before anything is decided, a market analysis is also recommended not only of "sticker price" student fees but also net fees after financial aid.

Assuming that these actions are successful, McKinley College can then turn to long-term budget challenges.

The current budgeting process is too centralized. The dominance of the chief financial officer probably overlooks crucial academic and student affairs issues, especially in the absence of a strategic plan. The president's low profile in budget presentation sends the wrong signal that the budget is a financial summary rather than a series of substantive decisions about the key functions of the institution. The budget should be a recommendation from the president to the board.

A participative budgeting process could build on an inclusive strategic planning process, possibly co-chaired by a faculty member and the chief financial officer. This would help everyone grasp underlying fiscal constraints and possibly inspire innovative thinking. The budget committee should have two or three faculty members, an administrator, one support-staff member, two students (one traditional and one adult), and the academic dean and chief advancement officer.

Alternative financial planning models that mirror the current recommendations of the board committees would be educational. What would happen to financial equilibrium if the institution adopted every board committee's wish list? What trade-offs are possible among financial aid, staff compensation, endowment spending, and other variables? The development of a range of fiscal scenarios now, consistent with the strategic plan, might avoid or minimize "silo" thinking in the event of future fiscal catastrophes and windfalls.

Adherence to the targets within competitor markets will be important. Rather than set arbitrary increases or decreases, McKinley should explain budget changes in faculty salaries and other large expense items in terms of their impact on the targets. The same market-driven logic and explanation should cover tuition and other revenue rises.

For current and prospective students and parents, McKinley should repeatedly and clearly explain the difference between college cost (cost of education), price (what students are asked to pay in theory), and net price (what students actually pay in practice after financial aid). This is especially crucial in this case given the stiff competition from lower cost public institutions.

The college should arrange to assess administrative programs for efficiency and support of the academic program. The chief financial officer might employ outside reviewers to examine such key business processes as course registration, counseling and health services, housing, and food services. Additionally, the chief executive and others can develop targeted ratios for staffing such as staff-to-faculty and staff-to-students, with the latter resembling the more classic student-to-faculty ratio.

President Hanna and the board must be seen as leading any retrenchment program that precedes or follows planning and budgeting. Providing them and the campus with as much accurate and understandable data as possible is essential so that rumor and myth do not replace the facts.

Retrenchment: Summary

Colleges and universities periodically confront financial shortfalls or even crises from economic downturns, enrollment drops, state-aid cuts, and other circumstances. Operating-budget deficits, increasingly higher rates of tuition discounting, and drops in student enrollment are among the surest warning signs of financial difficulty. Retrenchment in response to financial distress heightens the importance of good budgeting and financial planning. *Still, retrenchment also offers opportunities for change that would be impossible when the budget is stable.*

What principles should guide retrenchment? They center on attention to the mission, prioritization of cutting expenses before trying to raise revenue, reducing administrative before academic costs, focusing on transparency and community involvement, and exhibiting strong leadership from the president and board. Retrenchment proceeds in stages depending on the severity of the budget problem. Relatively easy cuts are made and expenses deferred when the problem is new or minor. At the other extreme, programs or even the institution may be closed when the problem is chronic and catastrophic.

Retrenchment at McKinley College: Commentary

Exhibit 8.1 suggests that McKinley followed few of the principles of retrenchment, judging by the chief financial officer's recommendations and the ensuing trustee debate. The analysis below follows the principles in the order they are numbered on the exhibit.

1. **YES.** Retrenchment is based on hard evidence that includes soaring financial-aid and utilities costs, a drop in endowment market value, and no position control, which has led to overstaffing and excess compensation costs.

2. **NO.** Because there is no strategic plan, the mission and strategic plan could not influence retrenchment.

3. **NO.** Except for enrollment increases, McKinley is not considering how to deal with the short-term crisis while acknowledging the possibility of future growth. In fact, the layoffs of staff and elimination of athletic teams, for example, are directly contrary to this principle. What about furloughs or job sharing for the staff or temporary shifting of teams from intercollegiate status to intramural or club status?

Exhibit 8.1 : Retrenchment Worksheet

	YES	NO
1. Retrenchment is based on hard evidence of actual or potential declines in public support, customers or clients, finances, and similar indicators.	■	☐
2. Mission and strategic plan significantly influence the retrenchment effort.	☐	■
3. Retrenchment planning and implementation considers the possibility of future growth.	☐	■
4. Retrenchment is not a "quick fix." Rather, it is a multiyear effort, involving both organizational and cultural changes.	☐	■
5. Retrenchment cuts costs before trying to increase revenues.	☐	■
6. Across-the-board reductions are minimized.	☐	■
7. "Growth by substitution": some programs develop or expand at the expense of others.	☐	■
8. Retrenchment recognizes that more revenues often mean higher costs.	☐	■
9. Issues of quality are as important in retrenchment as issues of revenue or costs.	☐	■
10. Persons or groups potentially affected by retrenchment participate in making key decisions.	☐	■
11. Trustees and administration are viewed as actively supporting the retrenchment effort.	☐	■
12. Retrenchment decisions are disseminated immediately and widely using a variety of media and methods.	☐	■

4. **NO.** The recommendations seem very short term (except for the enrollment growth), and no consideration is given to underlying organizational or cultural changes. What about the 80 academic programs that McKinley is trying to deliver?

5. **NO.** Many budget recommendations are revenue driven, such as those for enrollment growth and the boost in endowment spending. That the chief financial officer listed these recommendations first suggests the priority of added revenues over fewer expenses.

6. **NO.** The recommendations specifically include a 2 percent across-the-board cut and layoffs that do not mention a strategy or logic governing which positions will be eliminated.

7. **NO.** The recommendations do not stipulate any thought of growth by substitution, although program growth at the expense of other programs might well be the result of the faculty and staff layoffs and across-the-board cuts.

8. **NO.** In terms of the hike in student fees and fee revenue, no mention is made of the related increase in financial aid. The same is true, albeit only on the expense side, when cost savings from layoffs are recommended without an analysis of associated severance costs.

9. **NO.** None of the recommendations cites effects on student learning, graduation rates, accreditation, or other quality measures.

10. **NO.** This is a top-down process involving the president, academic dean, chief financial officer, and trustees without significant community input.

11. **NO.** Exactly the opposite occurred. The trustees and the administration are arguing among themselves about the appropriate responses to the budget crisis.

12. **NO**, or **not yet**. Because the case ends before the trustees made any decisions about the best ways to retrench, there were no decisions to announce.

Conclusion

Colleges and universities play a key role in providing the knowledge, research, and service that leaders, workers, and citizens need to meet the demands of the 21st century. They operate in a world of continuous change and challenges ranging from demographics and economics to globalization and technology. Strategic thinking demands that boards and chief executives take into account mission and core values, longstanding strengths, future trends, and unique opportunities. It is about exercising leadership in choosing priorities, obtaining political and financial support, and communicating intentions and results. It is about facing facts and encouraging continuous assessment and the use of data for improvement. It is as important to acknowledge shortcomings as much as it is to trumpet successes.

Strategic thinking is also about tethering aspirations to reality by a comprehensive strategic plan, long-range financial plan, and the annual budget. No strategic plan is ever complete if it does not identify how much it will cost and who will pay for it. No budget is complete unless its recommendations are justified by the institution's strategic plan.

Strategic thinking in higher education embraces not only intelligent content but also inclusive processes. A plan does not sell itself, nor does any budget. Gaining buy-in and support involves careful attention to how the plan and budget are developed. The ultimate aim is to build a consensual vision for the institution and efficient means to implement and achieve that vision. Many external and internal constituencies — especially faculty, staff, and students — hold major interests in the institution's future. They often possess crucial expertise and perspectives. They seek significant influence over how the plan is shaped and the budget is funded, and they should have it. They need abundant, clear information and transparent processes. Such methods go a long way to ensure engaged participation, which in turn ensures not only that colleges and universities make strategic decisions in the "right way" but also, and most important, that they make the right decisions.

Index

About the Author

Kent John Chabotar is president of Guilford College in Greensboro, N.C., where he is also a professor of political science. From 1991-2002, Kent was vice president for finance and administration and treasurer of Bowdoin College in Brunswick, Me., and senior lecturer in the department of government and legal studies. He previously was on the faculty of the Harvard Graduate School of Education, the University of Massachusetts, and Michigan State University. He holds M.P.A. and Ph.D. degrees in public administration from the Maxwell School at Syracuse University.

Chabotar has served on the faculties of summer executive programs sponsored by the Harvard Institutes on Higher Education since 1983 and the Seminar for New Presidents. Based in part on his higher education teaching, the Council of Independent Colleges gave him its Academic Leadership Award in 2003. Chabotar consults widely with higher education institutions and arts organizations on such topics as strategy, financial management, training, retrenchment, and cost accounting.

Chabotar has written for such publications as *Trusteeship*, *Business Officer*, the *Journal of Higher Education*, *Change*, and *Planning for Higher Education*. He has presented at annual meetings of AGB, the American Association for Higher Education, the Council of Independent Colleges, and the National Association of Presidential Assistants in Higher Education as well as those of several arts-oriented organizations.